The *Art* of Public Speaking
Marketing & Humour

Published by Notram Publishing

4415 – 58 Avenue SE, Calgary, Alberta, T2C 1Y3

Phone: (403) 279 • 1000

Fax: (403) 257 • 2282

E-mail: marton.murphy@hotmail.com

Website: amalgamated.webstarts.com

First Edition

August 2012

17 16 15 14 13 12   —   1 2 3 4 5 6 7 8 9

Library and Archives Cataloguing in Publication

Murphy, Marton F., 1935–

The art of public speaking, marketing and humour : having success using words of wisdom / Marton F. Murphy

ISBN: 978 – 0 – 9916940 – 0 – 6

A CIP record will be applied for and will appear in future impressions of the book.

Front cover image: Doing business with a handshake. The author (left) is shown with his good friend of almost fifty years, Ross McIntyre back in the 1980s when both men were in their mid fifties. Both men started out from very humble beginnings to become two of the most successful individuals in Canada.

Printed in Canada by *Houghton Boston Printers & Lithographers*. Saskatoon, SK

The *Art* of Public Speaking Marketing & Humour

Having Success Using Words of Wisdom

MARTON F. MURPHY

NOTRAM PUBLISHING
Calgary, Alberta

Acknowledgments

I would like to thank my parents, Dan and Helena Murphy, for their guidance during my formative years.

I would also like to thank Emily and Alex Douglas. Emily was my schoolteacher and she and Alex have been among my closest friends for more than fifty years. Between them, they showed me how to live and appreciate all people regardless of their race, ethnicity, or religion.

For all the knowledge and information I have gained over the years, I would like to extend my sincere appreciation to all those responsible for the content of the following publications: the *Calgary Herald*, *Calgary Sun*, *Globe and Mail*, *Maclean's*, *MoneySense*, *Bloomberg Businessweek* (formerly *BusinessWeek*), and *The Economist*.

Table of Contents

Public Speaking

Introduction to Public Speaking

O NE OF THE EARLIEST CONCLUSIONS concerning speeches is that Murphy's Law applies every bit as much to them as to any other institution: if anything can go wrong, it will. We should not expect everything to go off without a hitch. However, we are intelligent beings and people of planning and foresight. It is not unreasonable to expect that the majority of events that are under our control should be carried out with a minimum of fear, fuss, and distraction.

The fear of public speaking is widespread. An individual must learn to manage this fear effectively. Otherwise it will stop you from being able to speak in public.

Practice speaking in front of a mirror. Repeating the same speech until you are familiar with it allows you to become quite comfortable speaking on the particular subject. It is good to know the first few minutes of your speech or presentation and to rehearse until you feel comfortable with it. Practice in front of a mirror, reading the speech until you feel you know it by memory.

Writing your various topics on note cards that you can refer to easily, can be of help, as well as typing your speech in large print, so you can turn the pages and not lose track of what you are trying to say.

In order to overcome your fear when speaking, it is wise to look at your audience and if you see a particular person or two who are very interested in what you have to say, turn from left to right, and address your speech to these particular individuals. This will help you gain confidence when looking into the crowd and acquire the skills needed to become a more confident speaker. If you are speaking on a stage with footlights, these lights will blind you, leaving you unable to see the crowd. Therefore, you can look slightly above the footlights, so as not to be blinded by them, and make believe that you are speaking to yourself. This will help to control your fear of public speaking.

It is wise to bear in mind that you should let your enthusiasm and emotion show through. This is a way to communicate with your audience or on a one-to-one basis and allow you to be more persuasive, while at the same time being extremely positive in explaining what you do, or what your product has to offer, or how it is superior to anything else in the market place.

Fear of public speaking is perfectly normal and can be overcome rather easily. As John F. Kennedy said, "We have nothing to fear but fear itself." Therefore, if you repeat your speech a number of times until you are comfortable, you will find that your fear will have subsided.

Equipment and Supplies

When speaking to groups use a podium that sits square to the table and have the reading surface up to within eighteen inches of the eyes and at a slope of between twenty to thirty degrees. The lower edge should have a lip or be raised high enough to prevent papers from slipping off. It should also have proper lighting, either from above or attached, which directs light over the reading surface like a light over a painting, and not in the speaker's eyes.

Using a handheld microphone that might serve singers is not meant for public speakers. Only as a last resort should such equipment be considered.

Always make sure to wear suitable attire for the occasion. One can never go wrong with a conservative suit, shirt and tie. Your listeners should be listening to what you say and not thinking about where you got that yellow and green tie.

Make sure there are no distractions either around where you are speaking or in the hall. Usually, if there is a Master of Ceremonies he will control this. If one is not present, make sure that you have it as quiet as possible so the audience can hear you clearly.

An assistant who will help to arrange the meeting, the seating in the room, and is fully familiar with the crowd is a great asset. That person will be able to make suggestions as to what would generally be acceptable to the group you are speaking to and what sort of humour, if any, is suitable for the occasion.

Preparing your Speech

When considering how long you should speak, half an hour is usually more than sufficient. Be prepared to open with something special for the first several minutes, and then after you are nearly through with your speech it is good to have some humour to send your audience off in a happy frame of mind. It is a good idea to include in your speech quotations that your audience will find interesting.

It is wise to do a lot of homework on your presentation as your reputation and your ability to convince or make sales will depend on how good your presentation is. You must be able to have considerable information at hand and be able to persuade and motivate the people you are talking to. If you have some quotations from this book in your presentation to make it interesting, as well as some jokes, it will entertain your group. They may find you interesting and enjoyable to listen to, resulting in sales at the end of your presentation.

Remember to never talk at length, as people will get bored very quickly. When you are talking to a group, it is a good idea to think of them as friends, making it feel easier to speak to the group. When the author grew up, he had a neighbor who had never engaged in public speaking but planned to run for political office. His name was Mr. Curly. He would go to the barn in the evening and walk back and forth in front of his cattle during the long winter evenings, reciting his speech until he felt comfortable with it. Evidently, he felt that a group of cows were a better audience than no audience at all. They certainly never heckled him. He later went on to win political office and become a successful and entertaining speaker.

It is a good idea to use simple words and ones that you are able to pronounce easily. Do not use sayings such as "Like I said," or "In other words," as these sayings become boring to whomever you are speaking with. The author was president of a political writing and campaign manager for one of the most successful British politicians. This British politician was a parliamentarian for over fifty years and never lost an election. When speaking, if he wanted to get his point across he would say to the crowd, "I want to tell you, if I were in Ottawa I would make sure that farmers got treated fairly." He would stretch out the flat of his hands and if at a loss for words, he would repeat the previous phrase and emphasize it more clearly. As a rule, phrases such as this are left at a great importance in the minds of the people who are listening. This resulted in the public never forgetting this politician when it came time to vote, and he usually won with a big majority.

The author would like to emphasize quotations can be used effectively to demonstrate the thoughts of other people, which can give you more credibility and make you more interesting as you carry on your conversation.

If you are in a crowd, always be prepared if called upon, to get up and speak. As you are listening to the Master of Ceremonies or another speaker, always have a few words in the back of your mind ready to pass on to the audience as well as a few jokes to tell that pertain to the people in the group.

Always have a few well thought out questions in order that you can go to the microphone and ask a question pertaining to the issue at hand, delivering it in a slow clear voice so that people can hear you and relate to what you have to say. This will go a long way towards creating credibility.

When speaking to a group, always remember to have a quotation that is extremely interesting to a group. When a president of the United States stated, "Tear down that wall," people still remember the quotation quite clearly even after a third of a century. Another quotation that will never be forgotten was stated by the noted lawyer for O. J. Simpson's trial in California "If the glove doesn't fit, you must acquit." That was one of the main reasons for the lawyer's success — the glove in contention was too small for Mr. Simpson and this resulted in an acquittal in a murder charge. A Russian president is remembered for pounding his shoe on the table. This got him immediate attention and no one forgot his lecture at that particular meeting.

You may be a person that is capable of telling jokes, therefore the humour in this book will be of great help to you when meeting people and speaking to anyone in particular. If you do not possess this characteristic, it is wise just to read them several times for your own enjoyment and possible future use. This applies as well to the quotations. You will find that they are a resource that you can go back to over time and still find enjoyment when you read them for an additional time.

As a rule, you typically write your own speech. In order to get a good command of the English language, as well as pronunciation, the author found when he spent many months in camps in the oil or construction industry, that reading the Oxford and Webster's Dictionaries as well as both the Old and New Testament was beneficial. These books are extremely interesting reading and will give you a leg up when it comes to talking on a one-to-one basis or in a group.

Protocols in Public Speaking

Always be positive when speaking since you will find it easier when you speak on a positive note. Be enthusiastic as it enables you to convince whomever you are speaking to, whether in a crowd or individually, catches their attention and gets your message across.

When it is a function where you are required to give a toast, it may be wise when you raise your glass along with members of your audience to say an old Scandinavian toast of "Skoal," or some will use "Salute." If you are giving a toast and have lost your notes or forgotten the trend of what you are about to say, close your eyes for a moment, then continue on with the first thing that comes to mind. At a wedding for example, recall the bride as a child growing up and the things that you found amusing, mention how fortunate she was to get such a good husband. These generalities will get you through and save you from undue embarrassment.

If you are the Master of Ceremonies, it is wise to ask your speaker to talk for several minutes before he gets into the major part of his speech. Be prepared to state that you are pleased and honoured to introduce the speaker.

On occasion, a Master of Ceremonies will allow too many speakers and permit them to talk at length, usually allowing the meeting to drag on unnecessarily long. In one case in Saskatoon, Saskatchewan when it was nearly midnight, the Master of Ceremonies called on John Diefenbaker, a noted politician, to say a few words. Mr. Diefenbaker rose and said "When called upon to give my address at this time of night, I will do just that. At the moment, my address happens to be room number 436 at the Bessborough Hotel in Saskatoon. I fully intend to be in bed within the half hour. I thank you for inviting me to be with you on this sentimental occasion. It has been a pleasure to meet you all once again and now folks I bid you goodnight." With that he strode out of the room, followed shortly by the audience.

When introducing a speaker, if you are the Master of Ceremonies, always remind the audience what the speaker is about to say, how important it is to the group, list the speaker's qualifications to speak on a particular topic, make sure you are positive and persuasive, and make the speaker feel welcome. If you are asked to be Master of Ceremonies, make sure you get a list of any announcements that you are required to make, the names of the people you will be introducing to the audience, the name of the person or people responsible for putting the event together, and make sure to invite the people who have put on the meal (if there is one to be served) so they can be thanked and given credit for their work. Always ask someone who is familiar with the individual to pronounce the name for you if the names are difficult to pronounce. If you continue to have difficulty, write it down phonetically, so it is easy for you to pronounce and remember.

When asked to deliver a eulogy, make sure that you have something interesting to say. The author had a partner for many decades who was a very successful individual and also had a heart of gold. When the author was asked to speak at the memorial service, he mentioned that Mr. McLean was a daytime capitalist and a nighttime socialist. This light joke drew laughter from the crowd and helped break up the sadness of a somber affair. Another saying that the author has often used when speaking in public and writing letters is to state that Alberta and Canada would be a much better place if there were more people like Dr. Jones, or his dear friend Mr. McLean. This phrase is usually very touching and is not quickly forgotten.

When chairing a meeting, always remember to read Robert's Rules before the date of the event. You will need to know how to control the seating, and never let anyone dominate the discussion. Encourage everyone to join in and keep breaks to a minimum. Try not to go more than an hour, with two hours the maximum. Always start on time and carry on information from different meetings as if you are a seasoned chairman of political events. Remember to become comfortable in front of groups. The author has read an average of 5,000 pages a month, an achievement that has provided him with many hours, weeks, months, and years of enjoyable and interesting reading and all of which has helped him be knowledgeable on a large number of subjects. Being well read on a number of topics will assist you in answering a wide range of questions you may be confronted with in a meeting.

Dale Carnegie, one of the best-known individuals with regards to public speaking and training, 100 years ago said, "You must have earned the right to talk about your topic and you must be excited." That is an excellent approach. One of the most important sayings that the author has remembered from Dale Carnegie is "You always put the monkey on someone else's back." In other words, delegate authority. This is one of the most important concepts if you are in business—the ability to delegate and free yourself to more important jobs.

The author emphasizes that when instructing on salesmanship and public speaking to never go over your time limit and always pause after every key point. You always make eye contact with your audience in order to convince them that you are the best person for them to listen to or deal with. It is also wise in question and answer periods to not let someone from the audience who is trying to ask a question make a lengthy statement—this will bore people. It is the same when talking to an individual or a small number of people. If an individual continues at great length, cut in at a good time and make your point. This will save time and make money.

If you are questioned by the media in regards to a development or projects you are working on, always remember to never make your plans known to the media and public. There is an old cliché that Eaton's never told Simpsons their business. The author found this practice out the hard way when he was going to build a manufacturing plant in a small Saskatchewan town. When questioned by the media, he told them it was going to be a plant to manufacture asphalt products and that he was being given the rights to a substantial part of land in the town, which later became worth a large amount of money for a subdivision. Unfortunately, the media wrote up that the author's plans would ruin the town and the mayor and council called a special meeting to deny and renege on the piece of property and the permit to build a plant, costing the author a very large sum of money. It is always wise to be cautious around the media.

Just as location is extremely important to starting up a business, practice is particularly important for being a good public speaker and conversing with people on a regular basis. When the author was a teenager he set up a hockey net in his small backyard on a piece of ice, like Wayne Gretzky. He would spend several hours a day, providing the weather was suitable, shooting the puck at different areas in the hockey net. After doing this for several years, he taught his younger neighbor how to play hockey. This young lad went on to set up the Andrew's Hockey School of Excellence in Charlottetown, PEI and taught Sydney Crosby how to play hockey. These two gentlemen, Gretzky and Crosby, went on to become two of the greatest hockey players in the world. This is evidence that practice makes perfect, and that dedication is the key to success in any given walk of life.

Humour in Presentations

When telling jokes it is always important never to smile. That is what you expect from you audience. Always maintain a straight face as you as you tell several suitable jokes to provide some humour to your audience.

The author always remembers a political story told to him when he was a young man about sixty years ago. The storyteller told the author that Sir John A. McDonald came to Prince Edward Island and gave a speech along with Alexander McKenzie. The two gentlemen flipped coins and Mr. McKenzie won. Mr. MacDonald had been socializing with his fellow conservatives the night prior to the coin flip, and when it came time to speak after Mr. McKenzie there had been nothing available to quench his thirst, so he reached for a five-gallon pail that was being used for a waste paper basket and proceeded to empty his stomach into it. Never one to be lost for words, he stated to the audience "Ladies and gentlemen, I hope that Mr. McKenzie's speech did not upset your stomach like it did mine." This brought tears to the eyes of his audience, regardless of which political party. Mr. McDonald's great sense of humour got him through the day and a difficult spot.

– 2 –

How to Sell

A GREAT NUMBER OF PEOPLE HAVE SUGGESTED that the author has been successful in life, sales, marketing, and business, and that it would be a good idea to leave a legacy in the form of a book outlining how to be successful with selling.

It is always wise when attending meetings, particularly sales meetings, to have a handout outlining what the company does. Should it be an ordinary meeting, it is wise to exchange business cards.

It's a good idea to join civic organizations and get to know people from various walks of life and make contacts with others who may later become friends. The basic idea behind attending these meetings is to become known to those who count, to meet more prospects, make more contacts and sales, build relationships, and to create a positive reputation for yourself and your company. Some great civic organizations to join are Rotary, Kiwanis, Moose, Lions, Elks, or Eagle Clubs. These organizations consist of groups of individuals who provide services to their community. Other good groups to belong to and attend meetings are the Chamber of Commerce, because the people who attend are usually business people, Alumni meetings, if you have attended college or university, and cultural events. These are excellent places to attend, primarily because the attendees share common goals, ideas, and perspectives.

Doing charity work, community work, or volunteering are all excellent methods of networking. Trade shows are more expensive, but, if they pertain to business or government and you will have a chance to meet people who may become customers, it is wise to invest in this sort of event. Sports events are ideal places to take customers. You can enjoy the event and have a few hours to socialize. Happy hours are good for meeting for an hour with individuals in a relaxed atmosphere and chances are you will be able to make deals at that particular time or set the foundation for deals in the near future.

If you live in a neighborhood where there are a lot of people who are from the same walk of life as you are, there is also an opportunity to network. It is a good idea to utilize all people that you have met as references because word of mouth is much better than any other type of advertising. To make the most of any event, spend at least fifty percent of your time with people you don't know in order to broaden your base.

When starting out making sales calls or speaking to a number of people, it is always wise to pick who you think are the easiest individuals to convince in regards to your product. Ask questions of whomever you are talking with so that you too will be able to learn what exactly they are looking for from you. This will make it much easier to convince them and sell your product.

It is better to meet people face-to-face than making phone calls, but this is rather difficult if you live in an area such as Texas or in the Western Canadian provinces, areas with great distances between various communities and clients. The author has found that it is effective to phone, fax, or email the people you have decided you would like as future customers and send them a one-page outline of what you offer and what you do. In the first paragraph you should indicate what you offer, including prices, and in the second paragraph it is wise to outline, in detail, anything that is on sale and that may be a good deal for your prospective client. The final paragraph should be an outline of how long the company or family has been in business, as this will give them confidence that they are dealing with a reputable individual or company. It takes five minutes to make a call, and at the same time you can be sending an email or fax to the person you are talking to. Time is saved and you are making excellent use of your resources by doing two things at once.

When making phone calls to people, you should make the conversation personable so they will already feel that you are associated with them or their company. Unfortunately, a lot of individuals and businesses screen their calls by utilizing call display, resulting in ignoring calls from names or numbers they do not recognize.

Remember, all companies have to make sales in order to exist. Without customers and sales at the top, there is no work for any other employees in the company. The success of your company, or yourself, depends on selling and constantly expanding your business. Explain to your customers that by dealing with you they will make, as well as save money and that their association with you will be of great benefit to themselves or their companies.

In order to make sales, you must identify your target audience, establish a rapport, differentiate yourself from the competition, build credibility, identify their needs and get as much personal information as you can, which should result in the closing of a sale. Always be well prepared and ask intelligent questions, but also be prepared to listen because you may be able to learn more by listening to your customer. The customer is generally glad to explain what they want and the more details you receive, the better informed you are. Questions to ask, for example, are "Who do you currently purchase from?" "Are you satisfied?" "How much they are paying" "Is it possible to bid on your work or equipment" "Are you the person who makes the decisions?" "What could I do to persuade you to have us as a partner or client?" Your clients are closer to their market than most of the people you meet. They will know what they want in delivery, quality, etc.

It is important whether you are selling real estate, equipment, etc... to have a support system that creates an environment that causes other people to enjoy dealing with you. Bear in mind also, that if you do not take a risk, there is a good chance that you will not make a sale.

You have to be careful when dealing with people. An old saying the author learned from a neighbor fifty years ago is "People can be ashamed of you if you're poor, and jealous if you are rich, so try to dress and act the part that you are in the middle in order to create a relationship."

If you do not have a personal assistant and are using voicemail, it is extremely important to have your electronic answering service set on two rings, not eight. Ensure your message is brief and to the point. If your name is Murphy or your company is Murphy's International, your electronic greeting should be simple, such as "Murphy's, please leave a message." It is very frustrating when you phone and have to listen to six or eight rings followed by "We are not able to answer the phone" as you have already assumed you will have to leave a voicemail because no one answered. If the voicemail states a lengthy message such as "When you have listened to this message, please leave your number and hang up," you begin to wonder if they think you do not have enough intelligence to hang up the phone after you have left your message. If you do not have a proper voicemail, you could wind up losing a sale.

If you wish to be successful in sales or running a business, believe in yourself, create an environment that will lead to success, and associate with the right people. The old saying "Birds of a feather flock together" applies here.

Always keep up with the latest techniques in your field and always have an answer to any questions that you might be asked. In a good law school the first thing they will teach you is to think things through and never ask a question that you do not know part of the answer to. You must be aware of opportunity and take advantage of it immediately. Do not be worried about mistakes. Mistakes are what we learn from.

You should always be aware of investing your time advantageously and cognizant of what you can make on any particular deal. Perseverance and patients pays off. Only if you practice both will you be successful. Always have a positive attitude, ignore people who are negative, deal with people who are positive and that will become an asset to you and your business.

It has been reported that Edison failed five thousand times before he came up with a successful light bulb. In the present, Donald Trump has had many failures, but the end result is his becoming an outstanding success. You must be prepared to drive yourself to succeed. If you do not want success, then you will never be successful. Bear in mind that ten percent of people sell ninety percent of real estate. If you plan to be successful in real estate, you must be in the top ten percent of whatever market you choose. If you are not successful, be prepared to change your sales pitch, change the clientele that you are approaching, approach a friend and ask him to make suggestions on how you would be more successful, and stay with people who have already proven themselves as being very successful.

Make sure that you take time off in order maintain balance. Learning how to manage your time, whether you are working for yourself or another, is the most valuable asset in your life.

Do your homework and be prepared for the inevitable. Bear in mind the Boy Scouts motto is "Be prepared," and it has been thus for more than one hundred years. The author has become very familiar with the Boy Scouts as he has worked with them for nearly a third of a century and has seen first-hand the positive results of such a motto.

It is wise to have a company and to have your name registered so no one else can steal it down the road after you have put in a lot of hard work to build up the business. This happens too often to successful people.

When you are talking about yourself, Yogi Berra said, "It's not bragging when it's a fact." Always make sure your clients are happy and satisfied, and only then ask them if you could use their name as a referral. Earlier on, we spoke of how important it is to overcome your fear of public speaking and how important it is to improve your skills over time. This will cause people to listen to you and act upon what you say to them. It is also important to realize that the more you practice public speaking, the more confident you will become in your relations with your clients.

Have confidence. Confidence comes from doing your homework, being well prepared, and thinking positively. You must look forward with anticipation to making sales. This will make you even more positive and more determined. The more you achieve, the more you will want to win, the more you win, the more you will want to win and nothing breeds success as more success.

Overcome your fear and nervousness, take rejection in stride, and always maintain positivity with regard to the future. You will notice as you watch sports that the athletes always state in their interviews that they must stay focused and think positively. Your clients will rate you on your preparedness, desire to help, product knowledge, presentation, humour, positive attitude, and capability to establish rapport with clients, image, and ability to speak. They will also rate you on your sincerity and your reputation.

When you are feeling depressed and in the dumps, it is always important to regain your positive attitude whether it is through prayer, meeting with friends who help you build confidence, helping others through church or charity.

You need to have street smarts in business. Collin Smith, a very successful business man who owned sports teams and gravel pits, always stated "If you were playing sports and you could not beat your competition in the alleys, then you could not beat them on the ice in a hockey match."

You must enjoy what you are doing, if not, you should look for another field of work. Be prepared to put one hundred percent into your efforts and be prepared to go to extremes to succeed. The author is seventy-seven and is still working full days in business, politics, church community, and charities. Always be honest and maintain your integrity. Bear in mind that the devil is in the details.

If you follow the above guidelines, you will be happier than a pig in you know what and successful beyond your wildest dreams.

Read as much as you have time for. Subscribe to newspapers and magazines if you do not have time to read novels. Reader's Digest is a good suggested read. Read a broad range of magazine, novels, newspapers, and articles to increase your knowledge on various topics. National and Canadian Geographic can give you a worldwide knowledge of old and new events. In order to keep up on current events in America and worldwide, read the Global news or watch news channels over breakfast if you do not have much time to read.

A lot of books are authored so that the writer can speak to various groups across the country and charge large fees. The author of this book is simply writing it for the enjoyment of people across the world, and donates large sums of money to charities.

Another reason for reading this book is you want to turn your business from a money losing business into a very profitable one. The author first started in business nearly seventy years ago. His first successful business was in property maintenance filling potholes, asphalt paving, line marking, street sweeping, snow removal, and sanding. In order to get his first job he worked for a Catholic Church on the condition that the Clergymen would advertise that the author had done work on the property. If the person liked it, his number was in the bulletin so they could hire the company to do work for them. This approach gained a dozen clients. His second attempt was at a Protestant Church where he gained several dozen more clients from the same approach. The Minister in charge advised him to go ten blocks away to the Synagogue and do the same thing since the people who attended usually dealt in real estate and he would have a better chance to get business. He followed this advice. The service was held on a Saturday, and within two days, the author's company was booked solid for two years.

The author had worked for ten years in the oil industry and made a lot of friends and connections. When he was sent to Texas for a seminar, his group was asked if anyone could speak French. The author raised his hand and was sent in the company plane to Louisiana to buy a new type of drill rig for the company. The author bought the drill rigs and phoned his boss in Canada and, at the suggestion of the company pilot, asked if the oil exploration company would put up the money. They agreed to do so and in a matter of minutes the author found himself with a large quantity of drill rigs, financial support, employees, water trucks and a place to build many more drill rigs. This enabled the author to start up a highly successful drill business in the wintertime while still doing the parking lot and asphalt businesses during the summer.

Later on, the author met someone at a convention who suggested he enter the asphalt emulsion business, as there was a very high profit in it. He took the gentleman's advice and started building an asphalt emulsion plant and within a few years had fourteen plants from the Atlantic to the Pacific, all thanks to this gentleman who had passed on the information as well as the formulas and helped the author for decades. He was a very kind and generous individual.

Another opportunity came when the author was taking a week's holiday in Las Vegas and was passing the night away playing poker in the back of the room at one of the casinos where he met a gentleman. This fellow told the author that he had sold his business in the Northwest for ten million dollars and was now working for a very large company. He would provide the formula for a new type of crack-filler and if you owned asphalt emulsion plants you could produce it at a very low cost and make a very large profit. The author immediately flew back to Canada and started producing crack-filler, which had a very large profit and resulted in a high profit margin. This was all thanks to meeting someone socially and gaining them as a business informant.

The next opportunity came in the early 1980's from a man on a beach in Hawaii who outlined to the author how he could open up travel agencies in houses where stay-at-home mothers could sell travel for little to no overhead. The author decided that a much better way than this man's idea would be to put these travel agencies in insurance company offices as they already had spare desks and sometimes hundreds and thousands of clients who they could cross-sell from insurance to travel, while at the same time getting all the travel perks such as cruises, tours, hotels, and cars at fifty percent off. In a matter of months, a member of the author's staff sold over thirty franchises. Over the same period of time one of the largest travel agencies in North America was closing down dozens of branches. This proved to be another very successful venture until Mr. Gates of Microsoft got into the travel business with a company called Expedia. When this was rumored in the media, the author sold to a very large company with over one thousand branches in North America, keeping his travel benefits that had become very important to the author and his wife.

Over a period of years, the author invested in real estate, building his own properties with the profit of being his own contractor. He used profits from his previous businesses for further real-estate ventures. As a rule real estate and rents constantly increase year after year and are one of the best investments that any individual can make. The tips outlined above can be associated with his success and provide proof these tips are accurate because of his past. Anyone who follows the recipe outlined in this book can go nowhere but up and succeed beyond his or her wildest dreams.

Good luck, and all the best to the readers of this book!

Sincerely,

Marton Murphy
Calgary, Alberta
August, 2012

− 3 −
Quotations

Quotes and Comments for Business and Living

"A businessman who wants to be a politician is like a jockey who wants to be a horse."

"A car held together by paint, rust, and luck."

"A conservative is a liberal who got mugged. A liberal is a conservative who just got arrested."

"A cynic is one who knows the price of everything but the value of nothing."
— OSCAR WILDE

"A definition of big business is that greed, arrogance, and unscrupulous business practices are the way to do business."

"A desk is a dangerous place from which to watch the world."
— JOHN LE CARRE

"A failure is a man who has blundered but is not able to cash in on the experience."
— ELBERT HUBBARD

"A fool and his money are soon elected."
— WILL ROGERS

"A goal is just a dream with a deadline."

"A good police force is one that catches more crooks than it employs."

— ROBERT MARK

"A good small businessman must slow down to become a workaholic."

"A good small town newspaper, does not print papers, it prints money."

"A good speech is like a mini skirt, long enough to cover the essentials but short enough to be interesting."

"A house without books is like a house without windows. Tell me what you read, and I'll tell you what you know."

"A hundred years from now it will not matter how much money you had in the bank, car or house, but how you helped people and made the province and country a better place to live."

"A journey of a thousand miles begins with a single step."

— CONFUCIUS

"A lazy employee takes his vacation one hour at a time."

"A local gossip would make up a rumour if he did not hear one within an hour."

"A lot of business people should marry money or buy Lotto tickets."

"A lot of effort is as much a gamble as a plan."

"A lot of lawyers are like vultures ready to pounce on roadkill."

"A lot of people learn to work for money, but never to have money work for them."

"A man alone does not depend on anyone."

"A man is a success if he gets up in the morning and goes to bed at night and in between does what he wants to do."
— Bob Dylan

"A man is only as faithful as his options."

"A man who does not travel can be bigoted, mean, stubborn, narrow-minded, conceited and opinionated."
— Mark Twain

"A man who says what he means, and means what he says is a good friend."

"A man with a new idea is a crank, until the idea succeeds."
— Mark Twain

"A man with strong views can have a short fuse."

"A mistake is simply another way of doing things."
— Katharine Graham

"A narcissist is someone better looking than you are."
— Gore Vidal

"A person cannot control how he feels but can control how he acts."

"A person who does not read is no better than a person who cannot read."

"A person who knows nothing has opinions on everything."

"A politician can do anything he wants, but if he does not raise cash, he will not do it for long."

"A politician is a fellow who will lay down your life for his country."

— TEXAS GUINAN

"A politician's future is in the hands of his fellow citizens."

"A product for every purpose and a purpose in every product."

"A promise made is a debt unpaid."

— ROBERT SERVICE

"A real tough businessman can take a licking, but he always keeps on ticking, like a Timex."

— MATTIE McFINSKY

"A rising tide lifts some boats, and swamps others."

— WARREN BUFFET

"A round of golf sometimes ruins a good walk."

"A single player in a team sport never gets ahead."

"A small business is like a farm, always demanding time and labour."

"A squeaky wheel gets the grease, but if it squeaks too loud or too often it gets replaced."

"A statesman is a dead politician and we need more of them."

— BOB EDWARDS

"A successful life needs items such as family, community, and small business."

"A tax efficient business means we do not pay any."

"A threat to justice anywhere is a threat to justice everywhere."

"A week in politics or government can be a long time."

"A week is a long time in business."

— HAROLD WILSON

"A window of opportunity never opens itself."

"A woman drove me to drink, and I did not have the decency to thank her for it."

— W.C. FIELDS

"ABC's of Healthcare: Accountability, Be creative, and Cut bureaucracy."

"Ability is nothing without opportunity."

— NAPOLEON BONAPARTE

"Absence sharpens love but presence strengthens it."

"Acquiring money is a healthy way of life."

"After you have been clinically dead, always live with the threat of sudden death."

— MATTIE MCFINSKY

"Age is a problem only if you make it so."

"Age is a question of mind over matter, if you don't mind, it will not matter."

"Air passengers have the right to show up, pay up, line up, shut up, and sit up, and be treated like a nuisance."

"Alberta and Canada work better when more people can live their dreams instead of living nightmares."

"Albertans need a fair shot to get a fair share."

"All airlines problems were caused by deregulation."

"All around the wonder grew, that one small head could carry all he knew."

"All our life…is but a mass of habits."

— WILLIAM JAMES

"All the wealth in the world cannot buy a friend.

"All work and no play makes life very boring."

"Always behave like a duck: Keep calm and unruffled on the surface but paddle like the devil underneath."

— JACOB BRAUDE

"Always buy low and you will realize profits when you sell."

"Always drink scotch or rum so people can smell it and know you're a drunk and not stupid."

"Always keep the best address, even if you sleep in a basement."

— FAMOUS ARISTOCRAT

"Always try to cut some people some slack."

"Always try to stop discriminating against small companies and cutting special deals with big ones."

"Always try to turn misfortune into good fortune."

— MATTIE MCFINSKY

"An economist is an expert who will know tomorrow the things he predicted yesterday didn't happen today."

"An inspiration to all. If he can be a businessman, anyone can."
"An intelligent man's outrage reveals truth."

"An Irish wake and funeral is as much as social event, as a wedding or a farm fall exhibition."

"An undertaker is an expert on healthcare, somewhat like some political parties."

"Any successful person who does not use the word luck is not being honest."

— PAUL NEWMAN

"Anybody can sail in good weather, but it is hard to sail in rough weather."

"Anyone who tells you money cannot buy happiness clearly never had any."

"Anything worth having is worth stealing.

— W.C. FIELDS

"Anytime you can trade money for time, do so."

"Appendicitis will divert the mind from a toothache."

"As a businessman I never met a politician I really liked."

"Ask him a question and he can answer it before it even bounces."

"Asking an idiot a question is like asking a blind person to describe an elephant."

"At any given moment you can learn."

— TONY BENNETT

"At sixty-five nothing to do but eat well, relax, and fish."

— GORDIE HOWE

"Be an inspirational speaker, rather than a motivational speaker, as only you can motivate yourself."

"Be an outspoken advocate for the disadvantaged."

"Beauty is a short-lived tyranny."

— SOCRATES

"Before you diagnose yourself with depression or low self-esteem, first make sure that you are not, in fact, just surrounded by complete assholes."

— WILLIAM GIBSON

"Behind every great fortune lies a great crime."

"Being a perfect brown-noser can get you a leg up the greasy pole in government and big business."

"Being a perfectionist does not win friends."

"Better to live one day as a lion than a lifetime as a sheep."

"Betting is like liquor, you can make it illegal but not unpopular."

"Beware the law of unintended consequences when doing anything."

"Big business and government bureaucrats: name, blame, and shame them to get better government."

"Big business and governments favorite game is 'CYA'—cover your ass."

"Big business did not invent gouging but they perfected it."

"Big business leaders and politicians don't have stress, they give stress."

"Big business triumphs when good people do nothing."
— EDMUND BURKE

"Big business uses government as an ATM machine, putting money in and pulling out one hundred times what they put in, plus favours."

"Big business, big government: Might makes right."

"Big businesses are as cold and practical as a saw mill."
— PIERRE BURTON

"Big businesses treat shareholder's money as if it was their own, and if they do, they take it."

"Big companies are like big trees that hog all the sunlight and do not allow growth underneath."

"Big companies destroy reputations quickly with rumours more than with the truth."

"Big companies, if they can, set the rules of the game resulting in the odds of winning going up rapidly."

"Blessed are the flexible, for they shall never be bent out of shape."

"Blessed are those that laugh at themselves for they will never cease to be amused."

"Blessed is he who expects nothing, as he will not be disappointed."

— JONATHAN SWIFT

"Bonds are good if the country has no fiscal or trade deficits, and a high savings rate."

"Broad is the gate that leads to distractions, but narrow is the way to salvation."

"Building an empire is rewarding, but running one is not."

"Bureaucrats with lifetime tenure run their agencies like warlords unaccountable to anyone, even elected office."

"Business and sports need skills, reflexes, and judgment, but so does driving in a downtown."

"Business goes where invited and stays where appreciated."

"Business works on the bicycle theory, if you do not keep going forward you will fall on your butt."

"Business, not like a supertanker needing sixteen miles to go in reverse, must be like an Eskimo's kayak that can turn on a dime."

"Businessmen are like a lot of politicians, they use bait and switch tactics."

"Businessmen can only reach their potential by resisting the forces that attempt to pull them down."

"Camping is nature's way of promoting motels."

"Canada needs a new breath of air, and a fresh chance."

"Canada works hard and defies reality of history and geography."

"Canada: a peace loving, peace keeping country, with respect for human rights."

"Canada: peace, order, and good government."

"Canadians and Albertans are best at stirring up apathy."
— WILL WHITLAW

"Canadians do not kick a person when they are down, but help instead."

"Canadians have to ask: Are they happy with low interest rates, low unemployment, booming economy, or do they want change."

"Canadians in the army used to be peacekeepers and peacemakers."

"Capitalists can thank communist China for their successes."
"Careless words will always bode trouble."

"Cause cannot be divorced from effect."

"CEO stands for Chief Entertainment Officer."

"Challenges are opportunities."
— CONRAD BLACK

"Chance favours the prepared mind."

"Charity, what's in it for me? Happiness, satisfaction, a feeling of self worth, pride, a gift of your time and a sense of purpose."
                                        — MATTIE MCFINSKY

"Charles Goodyear developed the rubber tire and many more patents, but died in 1860, $200,000 in debt—proving geniuses do not always die rich."

"Charm if you have it, you do not need anything; and, if you do not have it, doesn't matter what else you have."

"Checking out many politicians is like peeling an onion skin, the more you peel the more you cry."

"Civilization begins with distillation."
                                        — WILLIAM FAULKNER

"Cleverness is the ability to conceal it."

"Clinton proved that cheating doesn't disqualify anyone from anything."

"Close only counts in horseshoes or hand grenades."

"Colleges are run for the benefit of the professors."
                                        — PETER THIEL

"Common sense is just a collection of prejudices acquired by eighteen."
                                        — ALBERT EINSTEIN

"Common sense means nothing in a courtroom, but is everything in real life."

"Communism without competition is as bad as capitalism without a conscience."

"Compromise is the cornerstone of business and politics."

"Computers make it easier to do a lot of things, but many of the things they make it easier to do don't need to be done."
— ANDY ROONEY

"Conceit may puff a man up, but can never prop him up."
— JOHN RUSKIN

"Condo sales pitches are tough. They are called running the gauntlet."

"Control the press and manage the flow of information to the people and tell them what you want to hear."

"Corporate rule begets corporate greed."

"Courage, Honor, Commitment."
— MOTTO OF THE US MARINES

"Courage, imagination, and passion can do the impossible."

"Creativity is intelligence having fun."
— ALBERT EINSTEIN

"Crime would not pay if the government ran it."

"Damn your principles, stick to your party."
— BENJAMIN DISRAELI

"Democracy is the road to socialism."

"Desperation is sometimes as powerful an inspirer as genius."
— BENJAMIN DISRAELI

"Destiny has two ways of crushing us—by refusing our wishes and by fulfilling them."

       — HENRI-FRÉDÉRIC AMIEL

"Destiny is not a matter of chance; it is a matter of choice. It is not a thing to be waited for; it is a thing to be achieved."

       — WILLIAM JENNINGS BRYAN

"Do not grant powers on the assumption that they will not be used."

       — LORD ACTON

"Do not let bigotry steal our hope and future."

       — ABRAHAM LINCOLN

"Do not let passions conflict with conscience or logic."

"Do not let the government think for you, because you are the government. Be cautious and concerned with a government that does not believe in democracy."

"Do not lie, cheat, or steal. All else is fair game."

       — JOHN McCAIN

"Do not mistake stubbornness for strength."

"Do not preach, screech or teach at politicians. Make fun of them. This they do not like."

"Do something every day to make people happy, even if it's only to leave them alone."

"Do unto others as you would have them do to you."

"Do unto others what they have done to you or to your friends."

"Do you want a hen that lays eggs, or a hen that crows?"
— William Aberhart

"Do you want to be an employee of people or an employer of people?"

"Do you work to live, or live to work?"

"Dogs do not usually bark at parked cars."

"Don't be possessed by your possessions."
— Lisl Steiner

"Don't be the kind of jerk whose wife does not want him and his mother will never take him back."

"Don't look back with regret, look back to learn."
— Bill Comrie

"Don't sleep in our bar, as we don't drink in your bed."

"Don't wear your religion on your sleeve, but let your religion give you strength and values."
— Abraham Lincoln

"Double standards are unbecoming and unacceptable."

"Dress shabbily and they remember the clothes. Dress neatly and they remember the person."

"Dubai is an oasis to trade, tourism and tolerance, created by vision and geography."

"Each time of life has its own kind of love."
— Leo Tolstoy

"Early to bed, early to rise, work like hell and advertise."

— TED TURNER

"Economic growth does not create lending. Lending does not create economic growth."

"Educate rather than legislate."

"Education is what you get when you read the fine print. Experience is what you get when you don't."

"Elections do not make democracy. Democracy makes elections."

"Employees and individuals conduct themselves with modesty, achievements, and gratitude, to their team with respect for all."

"Employees will only treat your customers as well as you treat them."

"Employers should think big, avoid mistakes, practice teamwork, hire people smarter than they are, and stay out of the press and spotlight."

"Enthusiasm is the father of excellence."

"Even when politicians admit they lie, nobody believes them."

"Every woman wants a bright, witty, gentle, compassionate man."

"Everyone talks about the weather, but nobody does anything about it."

— MARK TWAIN

"Everything has its place, and there's a place for everything."

"Everything in the country belongs to the big businesses or the rich families; otherwise it has no redeeming value."

"Everything Marx said about communism was false, but everything he said about capitalism was true."
— A NOTED RUSSIAN

"Exhilaration is that feeling you get just after a great idea hits you, and just before you realize what's wrong with it."
— REX HARRISON

"Experience is what you get when you do not get what you want."

"Experiencing nature for some is eating a garden salad."

"Failing health together with failing ambition makes your problems bigger."

"Failure is the opportunity to start over more intelligently."
— HENRY FORD
[who had two flops before he succeeded]

"False advertising by large corporations is not that they treat us as idiots, but that we may be idiots."

"Familiarity breeds contempt—and children."
— MARK TWAIN

"Federal government underfunds national student's education by half."

"Feeling like a Priest in a poor parish."

"Few things in life are as hard to put up with as a good example."

— MARK TWAIN

"Fight all battles on your own terms, not on others."

"Fight for principle rather than worry about your image."

"Figures lie and liars figure."

"Financial markets are more powerful than armies. Witness the rich and big business foreigners who take over a country."

"Find something you like to do and you will never work a day in your life."

"First generation starts the business, second generation grows the business, and third generation blows the business, as a rule."

"First: Faith, health, family, and friends…then money."

— SAM KOLIS

"Fish and house guests smell after three days."

— BENJAMIN FRANKLIN

"Flat tax in the US and Canada: Flatten it, fix it, or forget it."

"Flying is boring, loathsome, plus terrifying and a miserable experience."

— ORSON WELLS

"Food, fuel, finance. The three f's."

"For every action there is a reaction."

"For every sixty seconds you are upset, it is one minute of happiness you will never get back."

"For everything that lives is holy, life delights in life."

"For evil to triumph, good men have only to do nothing."

"For success, sprinkle water on a talent that has not yet blossomed and watch it bloom."

"Forgive your enemies, but never forget their names."
— The Kennedys

"Forty percent of women while during sex wonder when it will be over, thirty-nine percent hope it never ends, and twenty-one percent hope he has money, as they usually get paid first."

"Fox hunting is the unspeakable in pursuit of the inedible."

"Freedom is just another word for nothing else to lose."
— Bobby McGee

"Freedom to do what you enjoy, and enjoy what you do."

"Friends can have the different opinions but must have the same values."

"From disaster can come success and from successes, disaster."

"From one's mouth to God's ear."

"Get your facts first and then distort them as much as you please."
— Mark Twain

"Getting money from investors is important, but getting money from customers is more important."

"Girls were sugar and spice and everything nice, now they are strong as a bear and covered with hair."

"Give a man a fish and he eats for a day. Teach a man to fish and he eats for a lifetime. Show him more and he will own a chain of seafood restaurants."

"Give me your tired, your poor, your huddled masses.
— EMMA LAZARUS
[quote found on the *Statue of Liberty*]

"Give up what you enjoy and you may not live longer, but it will seem like you did."

"Giving people service, satisfaction with a smile instead of a smirk."

"Go hard, or go home."
— LANCE ARMSTRONG

"Go to bed when you're tired, work when you feel like it, eat when you're hungry, do what you want."
— ANCIENT ARABIC SAYING

"God protect me from my friends and I will take care of my enemies myself."

"God, grant me the serenity to accept the things I cannot change, the courage to change the things I can, and the wisdom to know the difference."
— ALCOHOLICS ANONYMOUS

"Gods greatest gift to us—the ability to help those who cannot help themselves."

"Going back in time is impossible, nothing is ever the same."

"Golfers are mad all the time, a good reason not to golf."

"Good and evil exist in all of us. Do not dwell on it."

"Good judgment comes from experience, and experience comes from poor judgment."

"Goods must be satisfactory or money promptly refunded."
— TIMOTHY EATON, 1869

"Governments are going to maintain control by consensus or by clout."

"Governments must protect people from other people, but they cannot protect people from themselves."

"Grass is green on the other side of the fence, but it's just as hard to cut."

"Gratitude is when memory is stored in the heart and not in the mind."
— LIONEL HAMPTON

"Gross national happiness is more important than gross national product."

"Growing old is a bad habit which a busy man has no time to form."
—ANDRE MAUROIS

"Half the money spent on ads is wasted, but the trouble is you do not know which half."

"Happiness does not lie in happiness, but in the achievement of it."

— Fyodor Dostoyevsky

"Happiness is a ball after which we run whenever it rolls, and we push it with our feet when it stops."

— Goethe

"Happiness is having a large loving and caring family, in another city."

"Having a judge on the bench fighting your case for you is the ideal scenario."

— An old lawyer

"He entered the scene like a stone thrown through a window."

"He had the wanderlust of an albatross."

"He is a man of sensitivity and sensibility."

"He is a man you do not want as your enemy. But you do not get to choose your enemies."

"He is like a thistle. You think you have gotten rid of him and he grows right back."

"He is like Harry Potter without the charisma."

"He was economical with the truth and always misrepresented the facts."

"He was so sharp I always worried he would cut himself."

"He who attacks everywhere attacks nowhere."
— Fredrick the Great

"He who is afraid to ask is ashamed of learning."
— old Danish proverb

"He would not let success go to his head. He would not let success even get near him."

"He's the type of guy who would not laugh at a joke, or tell one himself."

"Healthy habits not only add years to your life, but life to your years."

"Heart attacks and strokes can neither be predicted nor prevented."

"Hell hath no fury like a bureaucrat's scorn."

"High-priced houses, lost jobs, lost futures are no future: all due to corporate greed."

"History is the version of the past events that people have decided to agree upon."
— Napoleon Bonaparte

"History may be servitude, history may also be freedom."
— T.S. Elliot

"History never concludes, just pauses."

"History teaches us that men behave wisely once they have exhausted all other options."

"Honour is a harder master than the law."

— MARK TWAIN

"Hope for the best and expect the worst."

"Hope is the last of our feelings to wither and die."

"How do you learn to make a good decision? From always making bad ones."

"How to finance a business: collect your receivables fast and draw no salary."

"Hunters who carry loaded guns should be careful to walk and not run."

"I am a government worker so I'm used to doing little all day."

"I am a great believer in luck, and the harder I work the more luck I have."

— ABRAHAM LINCOLN

"I am handing you a republic, if you can keep it."

"I am my brother's keeper, I care for each and every one."

"I am no doctor, but the majority of people have a severe case of dumbness."

"I am not sure if our Lord was a liberal leader, he would be able to turn things around."

— BRENDON DUNFEE

"I ask you to help us let Alberta be Alberta again."

— LANGSTON HUGHES, 1930

"I cannot praise a fugitive or cloistered virtue, unexercised and unbreathed, that never sallies out and sees her adversary."

— John Milton

"I disapprove of what you say, but I will defend to the death your right to say it."

— Francois Voltaire

"I encourage debate but do not want to be confrontational."

— Mattie McFinsky

"I feel very humble but fortunately I have the strength of character to fight it."

"I hate stupidity and injustice."

— Sean Connery

"I hate war as only a soldier that has seen its brutality, its futility, and stupidity."

— General Dwight Eisenhower

"I have always tried to change things and people who are against change get angry."

— Bill Clinton

"I have come to the conclusion that politics is too serious a matter to be left to the politicians."

— Charles de Gaulle

"I have fought a good fight, I have finished my course, and I have kept the faith."

— Apostle Paul

"I have not failed; I've just found a thousand ways that do not work."

— Thomas Edison

"I have promises to keep and miles to go before I sleep."

— ROBERT FROST

"I have relatives and friends, some do nothing, and the others are their assistants."

"I have taken more out of whiskey than whiskey has ever taken out of me."

— WINSTON CHURCHILL

"I hope to be remembered as having the generosity of a child."

"I know what's going on, and I am going on."

"I never rode in a vehicle this fast that did not have a stewardess."

— CHAS DEIGHAN

"I offered my opponents a deal: "If they stop telling lies about me, I will stop telling the truth about them."

— ADLAI STEVENSON

"I swear to tell the truth as I know it, the whole truth as I believe it, and nothing but what I need you to know."

— POLITICIANS [IN GENERAL]

"I talk about those getting screwed and those doing the screwing."

"I taught him all he knows, but not everything I know."

"I thought I was God. Others did not agree."

"I work with two of the most unpredictable things in the world: Human nature and Mother nature."

— MATTIE McFINSKY

"I would need to see a politician walk on water in order to impress me."

"I would sooner have my enemies pissing inside my tent, than outside pissing in."

— Lyndon Johnson

"I'm not big on speeches, but I am on gratitude."

"Idle hands and minds create mischief and are the devils workshop."

"If a person does not want to help himself, no one can stop him."

— Sam Goldwyn

"If Americans want everything paid for, do not count on Social Security."

"If an idea's worth having once, it's worth having twice."

— Tom Stoppard

"If anybody takes exception to what I tell you, I stand corrected."

"If big business stops telling lies about small business, we will stop telling the truth about them."

— Mattie McFinsky

"If BS were money a lot of businesspeople would not have to work."

"If evolution really works, how come mothers only have two hands?"

— Milton Berle

"If he went to heaven he would be allergic to harps."

"If history repeats itself as a farce, fiction returns as journalism."

"If I am telling a lie it is because I believe I am telling the truth."
— PHIL GAGLARDI

"If I do not seem as morose and depressed as I should be, I'm sorry to disappoint you."

"If I dreaded to walk on water some would say that I could not swim."

"If I had known that all you need was a recorder and a pretty secretary, I would have been a lawyer."

"If I knew then what I know today, what has to be done to be a success in business, I would have never gotten into business in the first place."

"If I live to be one hundred, I can only improve the quality of my life, not the quantity."
— JOHN F. KENNEDY

"If I wrote a book it would be called: *The Wrath of Grapes*."
— MATTIE MCFINSKY

"If it is to be, is up to me."

"If no one ever took risks, Michelangelo would have painted the Sistine floor."
— NEIL SIMON

"If people did not sometimes do silly things, nothing intelligent would ever get done."
— LUDWIG WITTGENSTEIN

"If pregnancy were a book, they would cut out the last two chapters."

— Nora Ephron

"If the law is to protect us against idiots and bigots, who will us protect us against the law?"

"If the present tries to sit in judgment of the past it will lose the future."

— Winston Churchill

"If there is no alternative, there's no problem."

"If there's no answer, the question will linger."

"If time be of all things the most precious, wasting time must be the greatest prodigality."

— Benjamin Franklin

"If violence is not stopped in hockey they will need to print more tickets."

— Conn Smythe

"If wishes were horses, beggars would ride."

"If you aim to be kind, be careful."

"If you are going to insult a person try and do it politely."

— Winston Churchill

"If you are looking for ants, go to a picnic."

"If you are smart you'll learn from your own experiences; if you're really smart, you'll learn from other's experiences."

"If you can find the key to her or him [there will be a long life to use it]."

"If you can stick a finger in each ear they touch each other inside, your head is probably empty."

"If you cannot convince the people, confuse them."
— HARRY TRUMAN

"If you don't share the responsibility, you don't share the authority."

"If you drink you ruin your eating and if you eat you ruin your drinking."

"If you have a breakdown, keep on and create breakthroughs."

"If you have not suffered enough, you have the God given right to suffer some more."
— WILLIAM ABERHART

"If you keep score, no one wants to lose."

"If you learn one thing per day at a University, by graduation you will be full of rubbish."

"If you let little matters slide, you get a mountain of trouble."

"If you look old, it may be the miles and not the years."

"If you lose money you wind up without a pot or a place to squat."

"If you offer a job to politicians at two times their salary, from then on you own them."
— JACK ABRAMOFF

"If you sell your integrity for a dime, you cannot buy it back for a million dollars."

"If you want to buy, sell or borrow, I need to know."

"If you want to live in a nice house, play golf, work at your own pace, and travel at other people's expense, be sure to become a politician."

"If you're going to kick authority in the teeth, you might as well use two feet."

— KEITH RICHARDS

"In 2002 Canada is half the size of the roman empire at its peak."

"In a company you should work together and share together."

— MATTIE McFINSKY

"In a new area, proximity does not bestow membership."

"In any big company or government the left hand does not know what the right hand is doing."

"In big business, salespeople will never tell a lie if the truth will do more harm."

"In business bet on the jockey as well as the horse."

"In business you cannot manage what you cannot measure."

"In business you have to be aggressive, but not in a negative manner."

"In business you need a good risk-to-reward ratio."

"In Canada it is easy to make money, but very hard to get rich."

"In Canada we wanted French culture, British politics, US knowhow, but we got US culture, British knowhow, and French politics."

"In Canada, in Alberta civil servants supplement their pensions by going to work for big businesses."

"In government patronage comes before patriotism."

"In Ireland, I came among you and you took me in."

— HENRY FORD

"In Ireland, you would be a Priest or an IRA gunman; In Israel either a Rabbi or a Secret Service assassin."

"In Japan the spirits of the dead watch over the living."

"In law you can lose while winning, due to the high legal costs."

"In life do not hit on twenty-one, or else you will lose."

"In life it's not your aptitude but your attitude."

"In order to get into the lawyers hall of fame you have to sue."

"In Paris the streets and people both go in circles, also in Washington."

"In politics an apology would be an admission of error, and more grievous than the mistake itself."

"In politics do you want to be conservative, moderate, or socialist?"

"In politics sometimes it is your friends who cause you more trouble than your enemies."

"In politics you do not get what's coming to you, you get what you deserve."

— BOB RAE

"In politics, if you are going to overthrow the leader, you better succeed."

"In politics, sometimes you cannot speak or vote your conscience."

"In some cities police hand out tickets like confetti."

"In the Klondike, sellers of picks and shovels made money, but not many miners made money."

"In the majority of companies, the company is run by bribery, and religious groups by weirdos."

"In the UK and US natural abilities are derived by inheritance."

"In unity there is strength and financial success."

— P.J. PHALEN

"Income tax does not bother me as I have no income to be bothered with."

"Information, formality and attention to detail."

— LORD NELSON, 1805

"Insanity is doing the same thing over and over again and expecting a different result."

"Insanity is relative. It depends on who has who locked in the cage."

— RAY BADBURY

"Iraq is a full chapter while the rest of the issues are mere footnotes."

"Irishmen can take a licking, but keep on sticking to it."

"Is it something you would love to do, or something you would have loved to have done?"

"It ain't braggin' if you can do it."

— BABE RUTH

"It is a long road that has no ups or downs."

"It is a pity too few want too much."

"It is an unfortunate human failing that a full pocketbook often groans more loudly than an empty stomach."

— FRANKLIN D. ROOSEVELT

"It is better to die on your feet than live on your knees."

"It is better to lose an election than lose your soul."

"It is better to wear out than rust out."

"It is cruelly arbitrary to put all the play and learning into childhood, all the work into middle age, and all the regrets into old age."

— MARGARET MEAD

"It is difficult to make predictions, especially about the future."

"It is easy to ride a horse and conquer a country. It's more difficult to get off the horse and run the country."

"It is essential not as much to win, but to have fought well."

"It is important for salesmen to get information, make contacts, make connections, and get referrals."

"It is impossible to be a gentleman and a businessman sometimes."

"It is my rule never to lose my temper till it would be detrimental to keep it."

— SEAN O'CASEY

"It is nice to be important, but more important to be nice."

"It is nice to discuss the eternal subjects like whiskey and women."

"It is not easy when you are dying on your feet."

"It is not enough for big business to succeed; they must make sure their competitors fail."

"It is not for seasons, but for good reasons."

"It is not other people who heal us, but ourselves."

"It is not policies or programs, but principles that count."

"It is not the age of the person, it is the health of the person."

"It is not what you will die for, but what you will live for, how you live matters more than how you die."

"It is one of the most beautiful compensations of this life that no man can sincerely try to help another without helping himself."
— RALPH WALDO EMERSON

"It is only ninety-nine percent of the lawyers who are giving the rest a bad name."

"It is only the mind that separates men from animals."

"It is only when the tide goes out that you know who has been swimming naked."
— WARREN BUFFET

"It is so easy to be wrong and continue to be wrong when the cost of being wrong is paid for by others."

"It is the little things in life that make or break you."

"It is very difficult to look up to ladies who keep their ears to the ground."
— WINSTON CHURCHILL

"It matters in business not how fast you go, only that you keep going."

"It's a lot tougher to go from the back of the boat to the front in business because of regulations and competition."

"It's easier to be funny than to be serious."

"It's easier to change a man's religion than change his diet."
— MARGARET MEAD

"It's hard to figure out what people who do not think, are thinking."

"It's no fun being a politician if you do not drink."

"It's not personal, its business."

— Mafia motto

"It's not the size of the dog in the fight, but the size of the fight in the dog."

"It's not what you know but who you know."

"It's not where you came from, but where you're going."

"It's not where you go, but who you go with."

"Jails are worse than prisons, they are cement boxes."

"Jails should be repair shops not garbage dumps."

— Conrad Black

"Joy is the simplest form of gratitude."

— Karl Barth

"Just because someone or something is damaged you do not give it away."

"Keep active and you will be the world's oldest living teenager."

"Keep your friends close and your enemies closer."

"Kitchen renovations always cost double."

"Knowing your own darkness is the best method for dealing with the darkness's of other people."

— Carl Jung

"Knowledge of what is possible is the beginning of happiness."
— GEORGE SANTAYANA

"Law and justice are whatever the courts define them as."

"Law partners are allowed to keep what profits they bring in; that's overhead, and it's known as the [eat what you kill] system."

"Lead, follow, or get the heck out of the way."
— GEORGE WASHINGTON

"Learn that in life it is necessary to accept a small sacrifice in order to make great gain."

"Lessons in instant poverty are easy to come by."

"Let everyone sweep in front of his own door, and the whole world will be clean."
— JOHANN WOLFGANG VON GOETHE

"Let them hate us as long as they fear us."
— EMPEROR CALIGULA

"Life is always ahead of us, never behind us."

"Life is no bed of roses or there would be no need for the clergy or religion."

"Life is not measured by the breaths we take, but by the moments that take our breath away."

"Life is one long argument with death, no one wins and you cannot postpone the inevitable."

"Life is ten percent what you make it, and ninety percent how you take it."
— IRVING BERLIN

"Life is too short to spend it at the back of the line."

"Life never gets easier, but it does get better."

"Life past seventy-five is prime time."
— JANE FONDA

"Life, liberty, and the pursuit of happiness are very important."

"Live in your head."

"Live latterly as you grow older rather than vertically, deeper than wider."

"Long shot chances are like the Easter bunny running the Kentucky Derby."

"Look at things the way they should be, not the way they are."

"Loose tongues lose lawsuits and much more."

"Love comes and goes, but greed is constant."

"Love is better than anger, hope is better than fear, optimism is better than despair, therefore be loving, hopeful, and optimistic and we will all change the world."
— JACK LAYTON

"Love is never any better than the lover. Wicked people love wickedly, violent people love violently, weak people love weakly, and stupid people love stupidly."
— TONI MORRISON

"Love, like energy can never be destroyed, only broken down and transferred."

"Luck and genius is ninety-nine-percent perspiration and one percent inspiration."
— ALBERT EINSTEIN

"Make a lot of decisions, and then only some will be wrong."

"Making money is buy low, sell high, take advantage of the misfortunes of others, and later on you can create them."

"Many companies make money off investors rather than for them."

"Marriage is the relationship in which one person is always right and the other is always the husband."

"Martha Stewart got almost one year in jail for obstructing a government investigation, the injustice of the system."

"May the good Lord take a liking to you."
— ROY ROGERS

"Meetings are indispensable when you don't want to do anything."
— JOHN KENNETH

"Men are more often bribed by their loyalties and ambitions than by money."
— ROBERT H. JACKSON

"Mentally you are what you read. Physically you are what you eat."

"Middle class activism is a protest movement rather than a political force, objecting to waste and mismanagement."

"Moderation in all things, including moderation."

— Petronius

"Moderation is the last refuge of the union executive."

— Oscar Wilde

"Money doesn't matter when you have none, and it doesn't matter when you have a lot."

"Money is the best general purpose tool in the world."

"Money may not buy happiness, but I'd rather cry in a Jaguar than on a bus."

— Francoise Sagan

"Most human beings are quite likable if you don't see too much of them."

— Robert Wilson

"Most ideas are pragmatic not principled."

"Most people live with more hope than expectations."

"Most politicians and civil servants are highly selective with the statistics and facts."

"Most things that are wrong are illegal."

"My ambition is to have no ambition."

— George Harrison

"My life is my business and my business is my life."

— Martha Stewart

"Napoleon called Britain a nation of shopkeepers. Now it is a nation of gardeners."

"Never be afraid of excess, it prevents moderation from becoming a habit."
— SOMERSET MAUGHAM

"Never be ashamed of landing in life's bunkers if you have given it your best shot."

"Never change the vitality in your life for the length of it."
— ROSE KENNEDY

"Never explain and never complain."
— HENRY FORD

"Never forget or forgive, but after wars enemies still trade."

"Never forget the system is based on greed."

"Never give in. Never give up, to anyone."
— BILL CLINTON

"Never has one man shafted so many so quickly for so few. He gives new depth to the meaning of the word shallow."

"Never have your undertaker and your life insurance as the same guy."

"Never live for your age, but for your work."
— WILLIAM JEFFERSON

"Never make plans. Life is unpredictable, just like the weather."

"Never miss an opportunity, as water never flows under the same bridge twice."

"Never say you know a man until you have divided an inheritance with him."

— Johann Lavater

"Never second-guess inspiration."

— Flannery O'Connor

"Never start a war, but if in one, take no prisoners."

— Izzy Asper

"Never suffer from the disease of apathy, always be a leader."

"Never think you've seen the last of anything."

— Eudora Welty

"Never urinate in a well that you have to drink from later on."

"Never worry about money when you're poor, or when you're rich."

"Never, never, never give in."

— Winston Churchill

"New ideas are first ridiculed, opposed, and then accepted as self-evident."

"New York is not the big apple, but to a lot of people a bad apple because of the rich and infamous."

"Next time you plan a trip, remember the problems on your last trip."

"Next to trying and winning, the best thing is trying and failing."

— Lucy Maud Montgomery

"Nietzsche famously said whatever doesn't kill you makes you stronger. What he failed to stress is that it almost kills you."
— CONAN O'BRIEN

"No man can save his brother's soul or pay his brother's debt."

"No matter what you call a skunk it still smells."

"No more weddings. They are not tying the knots tight enough."

"No one ever went broke underestimating intelligence."

"No one would want a computer in their home."
— PRESIDENT OF DIGITAL EQUIPMENT, 1977

"Noise is an inspiration on sanity, and we live in very noisy times."
— JOAN BAEZ

"Not every right wing politician is a horse thief, but all horse thieves are right wing politicians."

"Nothing is more responsible for the good old days than a bad memory."
— FRANKLIN PIERCE

"Nothing recedes like success."
— WALTER WINCHELL

"Notice all the saints are dead."

"Old age is a great equalizer but death is the final equalizer."

"Once a man, twice a boy."

"One can never be too rich or too thin."

— DUCHESS OF WINDSOR

"One day's exposure to mountains is better than a cartload of books."

— JOHN MUIR

"One fears the worst and hopes for the best."

"One minute you are afraid you are dying, the next minute, you're afraid you're not."

"One must learn to be silent just as one must learn to talk."

— VICTORIA WOLFF

"One path leads to despair and utter hopelessness, the other to total extinction."

— WOODY ALLEN

"One sees clearly only with the heart. Anything essential is invisible to the eyes."

— ANTOINE DE SAINT-EXUPERY

"Only cream and jerks rise to the top."

— IRISH SAYING

"Opportunities are the head of problems."

"Ordinary folks are buying a roof over their heads. The well-off are buying a lifestyle."

"Our lives end when we stop speaking up for what we need."

— MARTIN LUTHER KING

"Our memories are card indexes consulted and then returned in disorder by authorities whom we do not control."

— CYRIL CONNOLLY

"Outsource your big business."

— RALPH NADER

"Patriotism is the last refuge of a scoundrel."

— SAMUEL JOHNSON

"PC and Republicans have the lethal reputation of selfishness."

"People are closest together when differences become farther apart."

"People are getting rich all over the place. Albertans wonder what it is costing them."

"People do not read *Businessweek*, *Time*, or *The Economist*, but read *Cosmopolitan*, *The National Inquirer*, *Playboy*, and *Penthouse* which is why they do not achieve greatness."

"People do not want to discuss open secrets."

"People look down on people who smoke, because they are in a casket."

"People marry people with ideas, but not enough with the courage and ethics to carry them out."

"People never lie as much as when after a hunt, during a war, or before an election."

— OTTO VON BISMARCK

"People outrage about outrageous policy." [POPE]

"People talk about the first day of your life. I look at every day as the last day of my life."

— MATTIE McFINSKY

"People think that he or she is nice and not clever, but they're clever sometimes and not nice."

"People want fair trade, not free trade."

"People who are left unheard must be heard."

— JOHN KERRY

"People who drink coffee and smoke two packs a day are puffing and peeing all day long."

"People who remain calm usually do not have all the facts."

"People who talk about the high road would not know it if it fell on them."

— JASON CLARK

"People working together are coming together for a common goal."

"Philanthropy is a term for the wielding of power for the rich."

"Picasso took only thirty minutes to do a sketch, but thirty years to learn how to sketch."

"Police are immune in court cases and misrepresent the facts constantly."

"Politicians are all crooks, and people are idiots."

— CONRAD BLACK

"Politicians are like diapers, you have to change them often for the same reason."

"Politicians are not running America, but ruining America."

"Politicians are people who, when they see light at the end of the tunnel, go out and buy some more tunnel."

— JOHN QUINTON

"Politicians are the same all over. They promise to build a bridge even where there is no river."

— NIKITA KHRUSHCHEV

"Politicians biggest disability is no backbone."

"Politicians gain power through manipulation, charisma, and emotion."

"Politicians sometimes can neither understand, compromise, nor sympathize."

"Politicians want to be a force, but turned out to be a farce."

"Politics and religions are now confrontational rather than conversational."

"Politics attracts people who wear masks, not people of substance and skills."

"Politics in the Maritimes is a disease, in Quebec a religion, in Ontario a business, in the Prairies a cause, and in B.C. entertainment."

"Politics is all about confrontation, conciliation, and compromise."

"Politics is like sex, it is all in the timing."
— WINSTON CHURCHILL

"Politics is not a political science."

"Politics is not like religious doctrine, it is more like buying a used car, always negotiable."

"Politics is show business for ugly people."

"Politics is the conduct of public affairs for private advantage."

"Politics is the gentle art of getting votes from the poor and campaign funds from the rich, by promising to protect each from the other."
— OSCAR AMERINGER

"Polls are for dogs."
— JOHN DIEFENBAKER

"Pride is an admission of weakness; it secretly fears all competition and dreads all rivals."
— ARCHBISHOP FULTON J. SHEEN

"Private equity bosses load companies with debt and fire workers to cut costs."

"Profit mightily by developing and reading, but contribute to own your real estate and resources."
— [said about Dubai, part of the UAE]

"Prosperity is a great teacher, adversity is always greater."

"Prosperity is not without many fears and distastes; adversity not without many comforts and hopes."
— FRANCIS BACON

"Public opinion is weak compared to our own private opinion."

"Quitters never win, and winners never quit."

"Read the tea leaves, or get out of stocks early."

"Remember the Prince of Darkness is a gentleman."

"Remember to expect the unexpected each day."

"Research and nonstop marketing are two keys to success."

"Resistance is not a sin, use common sense to change your mind."

"Respect, confidence, conviction, dedication, spirituality, and giving."

— MUHAMMAD ALI

"Responsibility when it is necessary, not when it is convenient."

"Rich is about want, not need."

"Rich people having problems that money cannot solve."

"Rome was not built in a day, only because the oil companies were not in charge."

"Rude, righteous, ruthless, right wing, rednecks are known as the 5 R's."

"Running a small business is like herding cats, very unpredictable."

— MATTIE MCFINSKY

"Sailing—all the comforts of a jail plus the chance of drowning."
— SAMUEL JOHNSON

"Sailing is okay if you don't mind being wet, cold, hungry, seasick, and frightened, all at once."

"Sanity is a cozy lie."
— SUSAN SONTAG

"Self-pity is our worst enemy, and if we yield to it, we can never do anything wise in this world."
— HELEN KELLER

"Sending anything to a civil servant is like sprinkling water on a duck, little or no effect."

"Seniors have a lot of friends. If they only knew they are not alone."

"Separation is like losing your virginity, if done right it can be very pleasurable."

"Setting a good example for children takes all the fun out of middle age."

"Sex is like eating peanuts, you keep doing it and you never get tired."
— ALAN GREENSPAN

"Shareholders meetings are like kissing your sister or a visit to the dentist, you do not like them but they are necessary."

"She never looked in the mirror to see the ravages of beauty, as there was no beauty to ravage."
— SOPHIA PETRILLO [*The Golden Girls*]

"Show business is not so much 'dog eats dog' as 'dog doesn't return other dog's phone calls."
                                        — WOODY ALLEN

"Show me a hill, and I will show you a tragedy."
                                        — SCOTT FITZGERALD

"Show me a man who enjoys college and I will show you a bully or a bore."

"Show what God would do, if he only had the money."

"Silence is the unbearable repartee."
                                        — G.K. CHESTERTON

"Simple's the most sophisticated thing of all."
                                        — INA GARTEN

"Since I started heart medication I am much more tolerant of people like you."

"Since others have to tolerate my weakness, I should tolerate theirs."
                                        — WILLIAM WHITE

"Sir, my concern is not whether God is on our side. My greatest concern is to be on God's side, for God is always right."
                                        — ABRAHAM LINCOLN

"Slower than a cat covering crap on a rock on a rainy and windy day."

"Small business needs a tailwind not a headwind."

"Smallpox is natural, vaccine is not."
                                        — OGDEN NASH

"Smart businessmen mean money, methods, motivation."

"Some businessmen charge very high prices, then slash with deep discounts."

"Some cities have potholes so big you can fish in them after it rains."

"Some defeats are only installments to victory."
— Jacob Riis

"Some doctors are a conveyor belt to the drug companies."

"Some have neither fact nor tact."

"Some Irish are like donkeys, good for very hard work."

"Some lawyers do nothing but specialize in high-billable hours."

"Some major families control politics, the economy, and the media in their provinces."

"Some men look like a gorilla and dress like an organ grinder's monkey."

"Some neither lead, nor do they follow."

"Some of our businesspeople need both salvation and rehabilitation."

"Some people are incapable of stealing rocks from a quarry."

"Some people have been sitting on the fence so long that they have pickets up their butt."

"Some people have charisma like a cardboard box, one oar out of the water, and a dipstick that does not touch the oil."

"Some people lose honour, fortunes, reputation, as well as their heads."

"Some people only tell the truth when it sounds good, and when a lie does not fit."

"Some people say we should save more and work longer, therefore destroying our standard of living."

"Some people see the world in only one way, their own."

"Some people yell like a demented parrot."

"Some people's stock suggestions should be warnings, not tips."

"Some peoples' statements are factually inaccurate, and I'm sorry to say, very offensive."

"Some politicians have a brain that is overactive and will overheat before it overachieves."

"Some questions must be asked, but not always answered."

"Someone in my family had to be weird, and I guess I was elected."

"Sometimes doctors and police have a blue wall of silence."

"Sometimes one has only to pose the question to know the answer."

"Sometimes politicians and bureaucrats fear losing power and perks."

"Sometimes you can hire better than you can sire."

"Speak and lead with your head, not your heart."

"Speak with optimism, resolution, and full of substance."

"Statistics are like a bikini, what they conceal is often more interesting than what they reveal."

"Statistics show seventy percent of athletes divorce after retirement."

"Stick a shovel into the ground almost anywhere and some horrible thing or other will come to light."
— MARGARET ATWOOD

"Stick to straight talk, straight facts, and straight values in life."

"Stock market turbulence equals stock market flatulence."

"Stocks: buy when others are selling and sell when others are greedily buying."
— JOHN TEMPLETON

"Stop lying or your nose will grow like Pinocchio."

"Stop oil speculation—SOS."

"Strength and wisdom are not opposing values."

"Success and failure can go from penthouse to outhouse."

"Success is when preparation and perseverance meets luck."

"Successful people are curious then ask questions. Failures tell you things all the time."

"Surprise me."

— BOB HOPE
[when asked where he wanted to be buried]

"Take a crash course to be a pilot."

"Take a rest. A field that has rested gives a beautiful crop."

"Talk is cheap because supply exceeds demand."

"Tax cuts for the rich are great, except the rest of Canadians are paying greatly for it, with cuts to senior care and the disabled."

"Teach people to think, not what to think."

"Television enables you to be entertained in your home by people you wouldn't have in your home."

— DAVID FROST

"Television is a medium because it is neither rare nor well done."

— ERNIE KOVACS

"Terror is a tactic, not an enemy."

"That is what they all say when they get caught with their hands in the cookie jar."

"That's the most fun I have had with my clothes on in years."

"The acquittal of some of the leaders of many nations was the greatest miscarriage of justice since the crucifixion of Christ."

"The average American translates greed into success as well as big business."

"The bar on bigotry is so high in some provinces that racists are accepted."

"The beaver said to the rabbit as they stared at the Hoover dam, No I did not build it, but it is based on an idea of mine."
— CHAS TOWNES

"The best thing in meeting new friends is the opportunity to make them old friends."

"The Canadian dream no longer exists."

"The cave you fear to enter holds the treasure you seek."
— JOSEPH CAMPBELL

"The center of culture in a small town often is the bars and the cafes."

"The corruption and influence of power and status in a society is valued more than character and integrity."

"The danger has passed because it has not yet arrived."

"The death penalty is archaic, barbaric, cruel, and unfair."

"The death penalty is on trial."
— BILL KURTIS

"The definition of an expert is somebody from out of town."
— MARK TWAIN

"The difference between what we are doing and what we are capable of doing would solve most of the world's problems."
— MAHATMA GANDHI

"The difficult takes time, the impossible just a little longer."

— motto of the US Air Force

"The doctor prescribed so many pills that they worked against each other, and nothing worked."

"The dog that chased the vehicles, knowing it was a funeral, ran alongside not barking."

"The dose makes the poison Paracelsus. If a drug is powerful enough, to help, it has the power to harm."

"The emptiness that comes to a man when old memories are full of realities of the past and reminders of the bleak future ahead."

"The enemy of my enemy is my friend."

— An old Middle-Eastern saying

"The first prize that life offers is the chance to work hard, at work worth doing."

— Teddy Roosevelt

"The first Whig was the devil."

— Samuel Johnson

"The flipside of winning is called losing."

"The four most important words in politics are 'up to a point.'"

— George Will

"The freedom of the press belongs to the owners."

"The friends you want are calm, considerate, and competent."

"The function of leadership is to produce more leaders, not more followers."

— RALPH NADER

"The gold ring does not come around very often, when it does you better be ready to grab it."

— JOHN F. KENNEDY

"The good die first, the rest are left to suffer."

— WILLIAM WORDSWORTH

"The government usually does nothing for us, but only to us."

"The great thing about getting older is that you don't lose all the other ages you've been."

— MADELEINE L'ENGLE

"The greatest and most important problems of life cannot be solved. They can only be outgrown."

— FRANK HERBERT

"The greatest boss is not the greatest leader, but the boss who gets others to do great things."

"The greatest lesson in life is to known that even fools are right sometimes."

— WINSTON CHURCHILL

"The hardest part is not thinking up a product, but in persistence and patience."

"The head of Nortel achieved a milestone in mismanagement."

"The heart of the most powerful tyrant trembles before the man who wants nothing for himself."

"The important thing in life is not the victory, it is the contest."

"The intellectual must be engaged."

"The journey is more important than the destination."
— ZEN SAYING

"The key to longevity is keeping your temper and your opinions to yourself."

"The last refuge of the insomniac is a sense of superiority over the sleeping world."
— LEONARD COHEN

"The liar's punishment is not in the least that he is not believed, but that he cannot believe anyone else."
— GEORGE BERNARD SHAW

"The Lord made water pretty to look at and fish in, but rum and whiskey are for drinking."

"The lowest form of humanity is to go to war and kill someone."

"The man who has been beaten is worth two who have not."
— VLADIMIR PUTIN

"The man who looks for security, even in the mind, is like a man who would rather chop off his limbs in order to have artificial ones which will give him no pain or trouble."
— HENRY MILLER

"The more some people pay, the more they think it is worth."
"The more you learn, the less you fear."
— JULIAN BARNES

"The most beautiful things in the world cannot be seen or even touched; they must be felt by the heart."

— HELEN KELLER

"The most truthful part of a newspaper is the advertisements."

— THOMAS JEFFERSON

"The mountains are calling and I must go."

— JOHN MUIR

"The mountains are the palaces of nature."

— LORD BARON

"The mountains, woods and lakes are lovely, dark and deep. He has kept his promises, done his work, and earned his sleep."

"The nation behaves well if it treats the natural resources as assets which it must increase for the next generation in value."

"The natural progress of things is for liberty to yield to governments to gain ground."

— THOMAS JEFFERSON

"The needy will inherit what is left of the earth that the rich has not stolen."

"The offense is not in being wrong; the offense is in doing wrong."

— JOHN DIEFENBAKER

"The older I get, the better I used to be."

— LEE TREVINO

"The only difference between genius and stupidity is that there is a limit to genius."

— ALBERT EINSTEIN

"The only difference between now and when he started school, is now he owes a lot of money."

"The only option is suicide but right now it is not necessary."

"The only place where success comes before work is in the dictionary."

"The only reasons some people get lost in thought is because it's unfamiliar territory."

— PAUL FIX

"The only thing inevitable after birth, is death and the time in between is short so it should not be wasted."

"The only thing we learn from history is that we learn nothing from history."

"The only thing worse than being talked about is not being talked about."

— OSCAR WILDE

"The only thing you can believe that you read in the newspapers is the date."

— CONRAD BLACK

"The only time some people are at peace is when they are at war."

"The only way not to think about money is to have a great deal of it."

— EDITH WHARTON

"The only way to get rid of temptation is to yield to it."

— OSCAR WILDE

"The outside of a person is not near as important as the inside."
— BISHOP JOHN HENRY

"The pain of war and politics is always local."

"The past is not dead, in most cases it is not even the past."

"The politician and wife both love the same man."

"The politician poses as a servant so he can become the master."
— CHARLES DE GAULLE

"The politicians worry about our jobs, when they're about to lose theirs."

"The poor rarely steal for necessities, rich steal for the embellishments."

"The present shouts, the future whispers."

"The price of doing the same old thing is far higher than the price of change."
— BILL CLINTON

"The promises of yesterday are the taxes of today."
— WILLIAM LYON MACKENZIE KING

"The purpose of politics is to generate hope."

"The question is, is the price worth the prize?"

"The reasonable man adapts himself to the world; the unreasonable man wants the world to adapt to him."
— GEORGE BERNARD SHAW

"The reports of my demise are very premature."

— MARK TWAIN

"The Republicans are the party that says government doesn't
work and then they get elected and prove it. The Democrats are
the party that says government will make you smarter, taller,
richer, and remove the crabgrass on your lawn."

— P.J. O'ROURKE

"The rich do not create a need they only satisfy it."

"The rich do not exist in a vacuum. They need a functioning
society around them to sustain their position. Widely unequal
societies do not function efficiently, and their economies are
neither stable nor sustainable. The evidence from history and
from around the modern world is unequivocal: There comes a
point when inequality spirals into economic dysfunction for the
whole society, and when it does, even the rich pay a steep price."

— JOSEPH STIGLITZ
[in *Vanity Fair* magazine]

"The right wing conservative can cause confrontation, conflicts,
and cutbacks."

"The sad truth is that most evil is done by people who never
make up their minds to be good or evil."

— HANNAH ARENDT

"The secret of getting ahead is getting started."

— MARK TWAIN

"The sign of intelligence is the ability to carry opposite thoughts
at the same time."

— SCOTT FITZGERALD

"The single most exciting thing you encounter in government is competence, because it's so rare."
— Senator Daniel Patrick Moynihan

"The Stone Age did not end for a lack of stone, and the Oil age will end long before the world runs out of oil."

"The strongest man is the one who stands alone. To rely on others is a weakness."

"The Swastika, is a five thousand year old symbol of peace."

"The things we hate about ourselves aren't more real than the things we like about ourselves."
— Ellen Goodman

"The tree of liberty is watered with the blood of patriots."
— old Irish saying

"The Treetown Kid, the no one from nowhere."

"The truth will set you free. But first, it will piss you off."
— Gloria Steinem

"The ultimate rulers of this country are the voters themselves."
— Franklin D. Roosevelt

"The US economy is moving to South Korea, China, etc."

"The value of an industry is inversely proportional to the number of awards it gives itself."
— David Burge

"The well-travelled appreciate the less travelled."

"The Wild West is a place on a map, not a way to live."

"The worst liar is someone who has spent their life telling the truth."

"There are no hopeless situations; there are only men who have grown hopeless about them."

— CLARE BOOTHE LUCE

"There are old businessmen and bold businessmen, but there are no old bold businessmen."

"There are people who have money and there are people who are rich."

— COCO CHANEL

"There are two motives for reading a book: one, that you can enjoy it; the other that you can boast about it."

— BERTRAND RUSSELL

"There is a fine line between lingering and loitering. We do not want to cross it."

"There is an old law that only the strong survive."

— LOUIS LAMOUR

"There is no future in pessimism."

"There is no more lovely, friendly, and charming relationship than a good marriage."

— MARTIN LUTHER KING

"There is no need for stores to give discounts as a lot of employees shoplift everything they need."

"There is no perception that is not full of memories."

— HENRI BERGSON

"There is no place like home, and it does not cost anything to get there."

"There is no such a thing as a stupid question, just a stupid answer."

"There is no such thing as absolute certainty, but there is assurance sufficient for the purposes of human life."
— JOHN STUART MILL

"There is nothing as important to a man as he approaches his door, knowing someone on the other side is waiting for the sound of his footsteps."

"There is nothing better than a friend, unless it is a friend with chocolate."
— CHARLES DICKENS

"There is nothing like staying at home for real comfort."
— JANE AUSTEN

"There is only one difference between a long life and a good dinner: in the dinner, the sweets come last."
— ROBERT LOUIS STEVENSON

"There is something more important than profit, and that is life."

"There must be a way to turn that guy's energy into an asset instead of a problem."
— PAUL MARTIN

"There's a sucker born every day."
— P.T. BARNUM

"There's more to life than making money, but not a lot more."

"There's nothing to fear but fear itself."

— JOHN F. KENNEDY

"They are unable to rekindle romance, because the fire is out and there is no kindling."

"They do not teach diplomacy at night school."

"Thinking of the future keeps me from thinking about the past and today."

"Thinking well of everyone is saintly but not sensible."

"Those in power have no incentive to think, and those who think have no power."

"Those that criticize tend to do less for others."

"Those who are too smart to engage in politics are punished by being governed by those who are dumber."

— PLATO

"Those who cannot remember the past are condemned to repeat it."

"Those who would sacrifice liberty for safety deserve neither."

— BENJAMIN FRANKLIN

"Though familiarity may not breed contempt, it takes the edge off admiration."

— WILLIAM HAZLITT

"Seven important parts of business, one: organization; two: evaluation; three: research and development; four: skills development; five: sales and marketing; six: new markets and expansion, and seven: maintaining customer service."

"Four things to never talk about: law, religion, whiskey, and romance."

"Time flies when you're having fun, and crawls when you have a toothache."

"Time is the only critic without personal ambition."
— JOHN STEINBECK

"To achieve long life: no stress, be friendly, eat well, exercise, no smoking, alcohol in moderation, have a nap or a rest every day, have friends."

"To appreciate life you need tough times and disappointments, hard work, and happiness."

"To avoid criticism say nothing, do nothing, be nothing."
— JUDGE CLARENCE THOMAS

"To be afraid is to behave as if the truth were not true."
— BAYARD RUSTIN

"To be successful in business you must get over the barriers of fear, and passivity.

"To be the owner of a small business in some provinces is not a position but a predicament."

"To die rich is to die disgraced."
— ANDREW CARNEGIE

"To find what Saskatchewan people have done, you have to go to Alberta."

"To live in a beautiful area, in a lovely home for a short time is better than to live elsewhere for a long time."
— MATTIE McFINSKY

"To most people power matters more than principle."
— MATTIE McFINSKY

"To pass the torch from one generation to the next is a real achievement."

"To succeed in business you need courage, capital, and confidence."

"To toast with non-alcoholic drinks is bad luck. The main reason is to drink alcohol."

"To try to be better is to be better."
— CHARLOTTE CUSHMAN

"To wolves and sheep, voting what's for dinner is hardly democracy."

"Too few people are honest, truthful, and intelligent."

"Too many people are indifferent, inexperienced, and incompetent, causing the downfall of America."

"Too much money colliding with too few brains."

"Too much or too little money can tear a family apart."

"Too much time spent on politics rather than good policies."
— STEVE CHASE

"Trailer and RV parks can be tin cans for tourists."
— Buyer-Beware

"Treason and terrorism is just a matter of timing, first a terrorist
and then a hero."
— Mattie McFinsky

"Treat your wife as a partner and not as a possession."

"Triple E Senate in Canada was started by Mattie McFinsky and
it was to mean Elected, Equal, and Effective. Mattie drew up the
first charter."

"Truth means nothing in court, or elsewhere. Only God knows
the truth."

"Try and retire from your own ambition."

"Try not to be successful but to be someone of value."
— Albert Einstein

"Try not to think of the future it comes too soon."
— Albert Einstein

"TV would last six months!"
— Darrel Zanuck, 1946

"Two smart people cannot agree all the time."

"Ugliness is in a way superior to beauty because it lasts."
— Serge Gainsbourg

"Unite and fight for what is right tonight."

"United States is a Christian nation, but so is hell."
— Mark Twain

"United we stand, divided we fall."

"Until politicians pay a price for neglecting the taxpayers and voters, there will be no change."

"US—freedom from fear, want, religion, and freedom of speech."

"US military—trained to kill, and kill we will."

"Use skill rather than appeal."

"Values are the very heart of any country."

"Vanity is a mortgage that must be deducted from the value of a man."

— OTTO VON BISMARCK

"Viagra and prune juice, if you take both you will not know whether you're coming or going."

"Victory belongs to those who have the resolution to attack. The defensive are doomed to defeat."

— RUSSIAN PROVERB

"War never determines who's right, just who's left."

— BERTRAND RUSSELL

"We achieve our goals when we take our eyes off the obstacles."

"We all cheer for David, but in the real world Goliath always wins."

— MATTIE McFINSKY

"We all choke. Winners know how to handle choking better than losers."

— JOHN MCENROE

"We all have one good book in us."

—RALPH WALDO EMERSON

"We are not here in life to see through each other, but to see each other through."

"We are often led to believe a lie when we really see eye to eye."

"We are serving the banks, rather than them serving us."

"We cannot change the cards we are dealt, just how we play the hand."

— RANDY PAUSCH

"We fight for the right and time to learn and think."

"We hang the petty thieves and appoint the great ones to public office."

— AESOP

"We have lived too long under Murphy's Law: Whatever can go wrong will. Let us change that for the better immediately."

"We make a living by what we get, but we make a life by what we give."

— WINSTON CHURCHILL

"We must always keep our friendships in a constant state of repair."

"We need faith before fear."

"We venture outward to venture inward."

"We're exporting America."

— Lou Dobbs

"Wealth does not trickle down, it trickles up."

"Weeds grow through asphalt, so it pays to keep trying."

"What can't be cured must be endured."

"What does a General do when the war is over? Get another government job."

"What holds most people back is greed, laziness, and stupidity."

"What is the difference between Quebecers and a canoe? A canoe tips."

"What looks more like tomorrow's problem is rarely the real problem when tomorrow rolls around."

— James Fallows

"What luck for leaders that voters do not think."

— Adolf Hitler

"What shapes a man's life, hereditary or environment?"

"What you want in a partner, horse or wife is staying quality."

"When a friend you need, they will always do a good deed."

"When a greeting is sent across from many miles you can't hear the wishes, you can't see the smiles, but you can sense the friendships that brought it so far to wish you well."

"When an Englishman speaks it is eloquent, when an Irishman speaks it is the gift of the gab."

"When asked if he had ignorance or apathy, he did not know, or did not care."

"When buying stocks, only the stock itself knows its own direction."

"When I am pushed, I shout."
— MATTIE MCFINSKY

"When I read the evils of drinking I gave up reading."
— HENRY YOUNGMAN

"When I was a boy I was told that anybody could become President; I am beginning to believe it."
— IRVING STONE

"When it comes to style over substance, style always wins."
— BRIAN MULRONEY

"When not getting your message across, you have the words right but not the tune."
— MARK TWAIN

"When preparation and opportunity meet, that is called luck."

"When saying something, say as little as possible as it may come back to haunt you."

"When sending a letter of thanks, the utmost compliment is, 'the province or state would be a much better place to live in if there were more people like you.'"

"When some people make a mistake they try to cover it, or justify it."

"When the circus came to town his mother hid him."

"When the cloudy pool of water settles, it becomes clear."

—BUDDHIST SAYING

"When the young bury the old, time heals the pain and sorrow, but when the process is reversed, the sorrow remains forever."

"When there is something you feel you have to do, your gut feeling is to do it as quick as possible."

— HARRY TRUMAN

"When things are good, they are not as good as you think, and when they are bad they are not as bad as you think."

"When working in the desert it gets so hot that the rocks sweat."

"When you come to a fork in the road, take it; remember, the future ain't what it used to be."

— YOGI BERRA

"When you forgive people, you gain strength and power."

"When you write off the liberals, they sometimes come back to bite you in the butt."

"When you're choosing the lesser of two evils, you are still choosing evil."

— RALPH NADER

"Where there is a will there is a way."

"Whiskey never hurt anyone, if it is left in the bottle."

"Who wanted their actors to talk?"

— Henry Warner

"Whoever has learned to be anxious in the right way has learned the ultimate."

— Soren Kierkegaard

"Whoever heard of opposition to a ranch foreman?"

— Nick Taylor

"Why do we need more prisons when the crooks are happy in politics and big business?"

"Will Rogers said he was more concerned about the return of his money than the return on his money."

"Winning is not everything, it is the only thing."

— Vince Lombardi

"Wit is a sword; it is meant to make people feel the point as well as see it."

— G.K. Chesterton

"With a lawyer it's not whether you win or lose, it's how much you can get away with charging."

"Woe to him who teaches men faster than they can learn."

— Will Durant

"Work twice as hard, work twice as long, and spend half as much."

— Mattie McFinsky

"Workers get the headaches and the bosses get the headlines."

"Working on a project such as this is like placing a layer of gold on a manure pile."

"Working wins when wishing will not."

"Worry is like a rocking chair: it gives you something to do but never gets you anywhere."

— ERMA BOMBECK

"Yell at your spouse and lose your house."

"Yesterday is a memory, tomorrow is a dream, today can be a nightmare."

"Yesterday no tears, tomorrow no fears."

"You can be husband and wife, but you cannot be friends if you do not share."

"You can bust your butt trying to achieve nirvana through inertia, but it will not work."

"You can delegate authority, but you cannot delegate responsibility."

"You can drive out nature with a pitchfork but she sometimes comes back with a vengeance."

"You can have democracy or corporate rule, you can't have both."

— RALPH NADER

"You can hurt yourself jumping on bandwagons."

"You can like people, but do not expect too much from them. There is good in the worst of us and bad in the best of us."

"You can make a life at the track, but you cannot make a living."

"You can make more money by saying 'I do' and marrying a rich person than you can by working for a lifetime."

"You can never enjoy spending money. You need stability, not show."

"You can never go back home, because you are not the same and neither is your old home."

"You can only lead where people want to follow."

"You can slide a lot farther on butter than on cinders."
— Mattie McFinsky

"You can slide further on BS than on sandpaper."

"You can tell a lot about a society by the way they treat their animals."

"You can tell his future if his financial planner is a bookie."

"You can tell when a politician is lying because their lips move."

"You can work hard and make more money, but it's better to make more free time."

"You can't go forward when you're looking in the rear view mirror.
— Pat Mesiti

"You cannot be both horse and jockey."

"You cannot beat somebody with a nobody."
— Abraham Lincoln

"You cannot control fate."

"You cannot legalize stupidity."

"You cannot legislate love."

"You cannot make an omelet without breaking some eggs."
— JOSEPH STALIN

"You cannot pass on wisdom to children; they have to learn the hard way."
— ERNEST HEMMINGWAY

"You cannot tell which way the train went by looking at the track."

"You cannot tow a safe after a hearse."
— FRENCH SAYING

"You could carve a stronger backbone out of a banana."

"You do not do charity to be thanked, but it is nice to be thanked for what you do."
— ANNE & BUD MCCAIG

"You do not get big to get better, you get better to get big."

"You do not get everything you pay for, but you pay higher for everything you get."

"You do not go to school or college to be a businessman or entrepreneur."

"You do not have to be in parliament to get things done."

"You don't slow down because you get old, you get old because you slow down."

"You get to the point where all you have to look forward to is your afternoon nap as you get older."

"You have a choice as long as you choose the choice you are given."

"You have to be smart enough to know the game, and dumb enough to think it is important."

"You know you're getting old when the candles cost more than the cake."

— Bob Hope

"You may be disturbed by the actions of others, but do not ever be discouraged by them."

"You may dress the shepherd in silk but he will still smell of the goat."

"You must do good, in order to do good in business."

"You must have principles but you must be practical as well."

"You need brains, brawn, and boldness in business."

"You need three things in life, something to do, someone to love, and something to look forward to."

"You never know what you will find, when you drag a hundred dollar bill through a trailer park."

"You never need a reason, just the means."

"You only live once, but if you do it right, once is enough."
— MAE WEST

"You only live once. You might as well have some fun at the same time."
— RICHARD BRANSON

"You try to be fearful when others are greedy, and try to be greedy when others are fearful."
— WARREN BUFFETT

"You want me to do something—tell me I can't do it."
— MAYA ANGELOU

"You worry when you do not have money, and you worry when you have money but they are different kinds of worry."

"Your body is like a temple, open day and night to everybody."
— SOPHIA PETRILLO [*The Golden Girls*]

"Your family and friends come first."

"Youth is a state of mind, not a time of life."

- 4 -
Jokes

THE REASON I HAVE INCLUDED HUMOUR IN THIS BOOK is that if you can get people to smile or laugh, it will put them at ease and create an atmosphere that is more conducive to making a sale and pave the way for the client to purchase your product or service. Should you decide to tell a joke, ensure that it is not a joke that is offensive to the people you are dealing with. Subjects that are safe to discuss are sports and the weather. In order to improve your humour, visit comedy clubs, watch comedy shows on television, and read joke books.

"The road to happiness is paved with humour."

For lexophiles, or lovers of words:

- A backwards poet writes inverse.
- A bicycle can't stand alone; it is two tired.
- A boiled egg is hard to beat.
- A calendar's days are numbered.
- A chicken crossing the road: poultry in motion.
- A dog gave birth to puppies near the road and was cited for littering.
- A hole has been found in the nudist camp wall. The police are looking into it.
- A rubber band pistol was confiscated from algebra class because it was a weapon of math disruption.
- A sign on the lawn at a drug rehabilitation center said: "Keep off the grass."
- A small boy swallowed some coins and was taken to a hospital. When his grandmother called to ask how he was, a nurse said, "No change yet."

- A will is a dead giveaway.
- Acupuncture: a jab well done.
- Atheism is a non-profit organization.
- Don't join dangerous cults: practice safe sects.
- He broke into song because he couldn't find the key.
- He had a photographic memory that was never developed.
- I thought I saw an eye doctor on an Alaskan island, but it turned out to be an optical Aleutian.
- I wondered why the baseball kept getting bigger. Then it hit me.
- If you jump off a Paris bridge, you are in Seine.
- Marathon runners with bad shoes suffer the agony of de feet.
- No matter how much you push the envelope, it'll still be stationary.
- Santa's helpers are subordinate clauses.
- She was only a whiskey maker, but he loved her still.
- The guy who fell onto an upholstery machine was fully recovered.
- The roundest knight at King Arthur's round table was Sir Cumference. He acquired his size from too much pi.
- The short fortune-teller who escaped from prison: a small medium at large.
- The soldier who survived mustard gas and pepper spray is now a seasoned veteran.
- Those who get too big for their britches will be exposed in the end.
- Time flies like an arrow; fruit flies like a banana.
- Two silk worms had a race. They ended up in a tie.
- When a clock is hungry it goes back for seconds.
- When she saw her first strands of gray hair, she thought she'd dye.
- When you've seen one shopping center you've seen a mall.
- You are stuck with your debt if you can't budge it.

AN apparently drunken cowboy lay sprawled across three entire seats in a posh Amarillo Theater. When the usher came by and noticed him he whispered to the cowboy, "Sorry sir, but you're only allowed one seat."

The cowboy just groaned but didn't even budge. The usher became more impatient and insistent: "Sir, if you don't get up from there I'm going to have to call the manager."

One again, the cowboy just groaned. The usher marched briskly back up the aisle, and in a moment returned with the manager. Together the two of them tried repeatedly to move the cowboy, but without success. He just laid there in a dazed stupor.

Finally they had enough and summoned the police. A Texas Ranger arrived, surveyed the situation briefly then asked, "Alright buddy what's your name?"

"Sam," the cowboy moaned.

"Where ya'll from, Sam?" asked the ranger.

With terrible pain in his voice, a grim expression and without moving a muscle Sam said, "The balcony."

∽

A farmer stopped by the local mechanic shop to have his truck fixed. They couldn't do it while he waited, so he said, as he didn't live far away, he would just walk home.

On the way home he stopped at the hardware store and bought a bucket and a gallon of paint. He then stopped by the feed store and picked up a couple of chickens and a goose. However, struggling outside the store he now had a problem—how to carry his all of his purchases home. While he was scratching his head he was approached by a little old lady who told him she was lost. She asked, "Can you tell me how to get to 1603 Mockingbird Lane?"

The farmer said, "Well, as a matter of fact, my farm is very close to that house, I would walk you there but I can't carry this lot."

The old lady suggested, "Why don't you put the can of paint in the bucket. Carry your bucket in one hand, put a chicken under each arm and carry the goose in your other hand?"

"Why thank you very much," he said and proceeded to walk the old girl home. On the way he says, "Let's take my short cut and go down this alley. We'll be there in no time." The little old lady looked him over cautiously then said, "I am a lonely widow without a husband to defend me. How do I know that when we get in the alley you won't hold me up against the wall, pull up my skirt, and have your way with me?"

The farmer said, "Holy smokes lady! I'm carrying a bucket, a gallon of paint, two chickens, and a goose. How in the world could I possibly hold you up against the wall and do that?"

The old lady replied, "Set the goose down, cover him with the bucket, put the paint on top of the bucket, and I'll hold the chickens."

∽

GEORGE was out shopping at the mall when he met his friend Kevin outside the jewellers. Kevin noticed that George had a small gift-wrapped box in his hand.

"So what've you just picked up, George?" Kevin asks.

"Well, now that you've been asking," replies George, "it's mine and the missus' anniversary tomorrow, and when I asked her this morning what she wanted for our special day she said, 'Oh, I don't know dear, just give me something with a lot of diamonds'."

"So what'd you get her?" Kevin asks.

George replied, smiling, "I bought her a deck of cards."

∽

TWO natives and I were walking through the woods. All of a sudden one of the natives ran up a hill to the mouth of a small cave. "Woooo!, Woooo!, Wooooo!" he called into the cave and listened closely until he heard an answering, "Woooo!, Woooo!, Wooooo! He then tore off his clothes and ran into the cave.

I was puzzled and asked the remaining native what it was all about. "Was he crazy or what?"

The native replied, "No, it is our custom during mating season when native men see a cave, they holler, 'Woooo!, Woooo!, Wooooo!', into an opening. If they get an answer back it means there is a beautiful woman in there waiting for us."

Just then they came upon another cave. The second native ran up to the cave, stopped, and hollered, "Woooo!, Woooo!, Wooooo!" Immediately there was the answer "Woooo!, Woooo!, Wooooo!", from deep inside. He also tore off his clothes and ran into the opening.

I wandered around in the woods for a while, and then spied a third large cave. As I looked in amazement at the size of the huge opening, I was thinking "How, Man! Look at the size of this cave! It's bigger than those the natives found. There must be some really big, fine women in this cave!"

I stood in front of the opening and hollered with all my might, "Woooo!, Woooo!, Wooooo!"

Like the others, I then heard an answering call, "Woooo!, Woooo!, Wooooo!" With a gleam in my eye and a smile on my face, I raced into the cave, tearing my clothes off as I ran. The following day, the headline of the local newspaper read: "NAKED ———— RUN OVER BY TRAIN"

APHORISM: A short, pointed sentence that expresses a wise or clever observation, or a general truth.

- The nicest thing about the future is…that it always starts tomorrow.
- Money will buy a fine dog, but only kindness will make him wag his tail.
- If you don't have a sense of humour, you probably don't have any sense at all.
- Seat belts are not as confining as wheelchairs.
- A good time to keep your mouth shut is when you're in deep water.
- How come it takes so little time for a child who is afraid of the dark to become a teenager who wants to stay out all night?

- Business conventions are important…because they demonstrate how many people a company can operate without.
- Why is it that at class reunions you feel younger than everyone else looks?
- Scratch a cat…and you will have a permanent job.
- No one has more driving ambition than the teenage boy who wants to buy a car.
- There are no new sins; just old ones that get more publicity.
- There are worse things than getting a call for a wrong number at 4:00 am—like, it could be the right number.
- No one ever says "It's only a game" when their team is winning.
- I've reached the age where 'happy hour' is a nap.
- Be careful about reading the fine print…there's no way you're going to like it.
- The trouble with bucket seats is that not everybody has the same size bucket.
- Do you realize that, in about 40 years, we'll have thousands of old ladies running around with tattoos? (And rap music will be the Golden Oldies!)
- Money can't buy happiness—but somehow it's more comfortable to cry in a Cadillac than in a Yugo.
- After 60, if you don't wake up aching in every joint, you're probably dead.
- Always be yourself because the people that matter don't mind, and the ones that mind don't matter.
- Life isn't tied with a bow, but it's still a gift.

↜

Someone asked the Dalai Lama what surprises him most. This was his response:

"Man, because he sacrifices his health in order to make money. Then he sacrifices money to recuperate his health, and then he is so anxious about the future that he does not enjoy the present; the result being that he does not live in the present or the future; He lives as if he's never going to die, and then he dies having never really lived."

&

WEATHER does something to you. The air is alive with the smell of leaves and flowers. It's interesting the way leaves turn colours, from yellow, red, golden, and then brown. Just like women.

Late fall is when the green leaves we loved so much turn to brown and our tans turn to pale. I don't want to criticize Mother Nature, she does the best she can, but wouldn't it be a lot smarter to have leaves fall up?

&

CHRISTMAS lights: They remind me of politicians.... They all hang together, half of them don't work, and the ones that do aren't very bright.

&

MCQUILLAN walked into a pub and ordered martini after martini, each time removing the olives and placing them in a jar.

When the jar was filled with olives and all the drinks consumed, the Irishman started to leave.

"S'cuse me," said a customer, who was puzzled over what McQuillan had done, "What was that all about?"

"Nothing," said the Irishman, "My wife just sent me out for a jar of olives!"

&

AN Irishman arrived at Heathrow Airport and wandered around the terminal with tears streaming down his cheeks. An airline employee asked him if he was already homesick.

"No," replied the Irishman, "I've lost all my luggage!"

"How'd that happen?"

"The friggin' cork fell out!" said the Irishman.

⤺

My buddy's missus left him last Thursday. She said she was going out for a pint of milk and never came back! I asked him how he was coping and he said, "Not bad, I've been using that powdered stuff."

⤺

Two Maritimers find a mirror in the road. The first one picks it up and says, "Lard Jasus I knows this face buy I can't put a name to it." The second picks it up and says, "You stupid bastard, It's me!"

⤺

The Maritimes have solved their own fuel problems. They imported fifty million tons of sand from the Arabs and they're going to drill for their own oil.

⤺

It was snowing heavily and blowing to the point that visibility was almost zero when the little Blonde got off work. She made her way to her car and wondered how she was going to make it home. She sat in her car while it warmed up and thought about her situation. She finally remembered her father's advice that if she got caught in a blizzard she should wait for a snowplow to come by and follow it. That way she would not get stuck in a snowdrift.

This made her feel much better and sure enough in a little while a snowplow went by and she started to follow it. As she followed the snowplow she was feeling very smug as they continued and she was not having any problems with the blizzard conditions.

After an hour had passed, she was somewhat surprised when the snowplow stopped and the driver got out and came back to her car and signaled for her to roll down her window. The snowplow driver wanted to know if she was alright, as she had been following him for a long time. She said that she was fine and told him of her daddy's advice to follow a plow when caught in a blizzard.

The driver replied that it was okay with him and she could continue if she wanted, but he was done with the Wal-Mart parking lot, and was going over to Sears next.

$\backsim$

THE Inuit Olympics were taking place in Duncan, British Columbia and the next competition was the Hammer Toss.

The first native up was representing Alberta. He grabs the hammer and tosses it two hundred and fifty yards.

"Holy cow, you have broken the world's record. How'd you do it?" he was asked. "My grandfather was an oilman, my father is an oilman, and I am an oilman. Have strong arms, throw hammer far."

The second native is representing British Columbia and he grabs the hammer and tosses it three hundred yards.

"You just broke the last guy's record. How'd you do it?" he is asked. "My grandfather was a logger, my father is a logger, and I am a logger. Strong arms, throw hammer far."

The third is representing Saskatchewan and he grabs the hammer and throws it three hundred seventy-five yards.

"Holy Moses, you just blew everyone away. How'd you do it?"

"My grandfather was on welfare, my father is on welfare, and I am on welfare. I was taught that if I ever see a tool, pick it up and throw it as far away as possible."

$\backsim$

THE teacher asked young Patrick Murphy, "What do you do at Christmas time?"

Patrick addressed the class: "Well, Ms. Jones, me and my twelve brothers and sister go to midnight mass and we sing hymns; then we come home very late and we put mince pies by the back door and hang up our stockings. Then, all very excited, we go to bed and wait for Father Christmas to come with all our toys."

"Very nice Patrick," she said. "Now, Jimmy Brown, what do you do at Christmas?"

"Well Ms. Jones, me and my sister also go to church with my mom and dad and we sing carols and we get home ever so late. We put cookies and milk by the chimney and we hang up our stockings. We hardly sleep waiting for Santa Clause to bring our presents."

Realizing there was a Jewish boy in the class and not wanting to leave him out of the discussion she asked, "Now, Isaac Cohen, what do you do at Christmas?"

Isaac said, "Well, it's the same thing every year. Dad comes home from the office, we all pile into the Rolls Royce, and then we drive to Dad's toy factory. When we get inside, we look at all the empty shelves and begin to sing: "What a Friend We Have in Jesus." Then we go to the Bahamas."

∽

A couple was celebrating fifty years together. Their three kids, all very successful, agreed to a Sunday dinner in their honour.

"Happy anniversary Mom and Dad!" gushed son number one. "Sorry I'm running late. I had an emergency at the hospital with a patient, you know how it is, and I didn't have time to get you a gift." "Not to worry," said the father, "The important thing is that we're all together today."

Son number two arrived and announced, "You and Mom look great, Dad. I just flew in from Los Angeles between depositions and didn't have time to shop for you." "It's nothing," said the father, "we're glad you were able to come."

Just then the daughter arrived. "Hello and happy anniversary! I'm sorry, but my boss is sending me out of town and I was really busy packing so I didn't have time to get you anything."

After they finished desert the father said, "There's something your mother and I have wanted to tell you for a long time. You see, we were really very poor. Despite this, we were able to send each of you to college. Throughout the years your mother and I knew that we loved each other very much, but we just never found the time to get married."

The three children gasped an all said, "You mean we're bastards?"

"Yep," said the father, "And cheap ones, too."

⤻

THREE Irishmen, Paddy, Sean, and Seamus, were stumbling home from the pub late one night and found themselves on the road that led right past the old graveyard.

"Hey, come have a look over here," says Paddy, "It's Michael O'Grady's grave, God bless his soul. He lived to the ripe old age of eighty-seven."

"That's nothing," says Sean, "Here's one named Patrick O'Toole. It says here that he was ninety-five when he died."

Just then, Seamus yells out, "Good god, here's a feller that got to be one hundred forty-five!"

"What was his name?" asks Paddy.

Seamus stumbles around a bit, awkwardly lights a match to see what else is on the stone marker and exclaims "Miles, from Dublin."

⤻

THE pharmacist walks into his store to find a guy leaning heavily against a wall. He asks the Maritime clerk: "What's with that guy over there by the wall?"

The clerk responds: "Well, he came in this morning to get something for his cough. I couldn't find cough syrup, so I gave him an entire bottle of laxative."

The pharmacist yells: "You idiot, you can't treat a cough with a laxative!"

The Maritime clerk responds: "Of course you can! Look at him, he's afraid to cough!"

A young Scottish lad and lass were sitting on a low stone wall, holding hands, gazing out over the loch. For several minutes they sat silently. Then finally the girl looked at the boy and said, "A penny for your thoughts, Angus."

"Well, uh, I was thinkin'… perhaps it's aboot time for a wee kiss." The girl blushed, then leaned over and kissed him lightly on the cheek.

Then he blushed. The two turned once again to gaze out over the loch. Minutes passed and the girl spoke again. "Another penny for your thoughts, Angus." "

Well, uh, I was thinkin' perhaps it's noo aboot time for a wee cuddle."

The girl blushed, then leaned over and cuddled him for a few seconds. Then he blushed. And the two turned once again to gaze out over the loch. After a while, she again said, "Another penny for your thoughts, Angus."

"Well, uh, I was thinkin' perhaps its aboot time you let me put my hand on your leg." The girl blushed, then took his hand and put it on her knee. Then he blushed. Then the two turned once again to gaze out over the loch before the girl spoke again, "Another penny for your thoughts, Angus."

The young man glanced down with a furled brow. "Well, noo," he said, 'my thoughts are a wee bit more serious this time.' "Really?" said the lass in a whisper, filled with anticipation. "Aye," said the lad, nodding.

The girl looked away in shyness, began to blush, and bit her lip in anticipation of the ultimate request.

Then he said, "Dae ye nae think it's aboot time ye paid me the first three pennies?"

↩

A retired man went into the Job Centre in Downtown Denver, Colorado, and saw a card advertising for a Gynaecologist's assistant. Interested, he went in and asked the clerk for details.

The clerk pulled up the file and read, "The job entails getting the ladies ready for the gynaecologist. You have to help the women out of their underwear, lay them down, and carefully wash their private regions, then apply shaving foam and gently shave off the hair, then rub in some soothing oils so they're ready for the gynaecologist's examination. The annual salary is $65,000, and you'll have to go to Billings, Montana."

"Good grief, is that where the job is?"

"No sir, that's where the end of the line is right now."

⌇

A social worker from a big city recently transferred to Grimsby, Ontario, a small community. This was on the first tour of her new territory when she came upon the tiniest cabin she had ever seen in her life.

Intrigued, she went up and knocked on the door. "Anybody home?" she asked.

"Yep." Came a kid's voice through the door.

"Is your father there?" asked the social worker.

"Pa? Nope, he left before Ma came in," said the kid.

"Well, is your mother there?" persisted the social worker.

"Ma?" Nope, she left just before I got here," said the kid.

"But," protested the social worker, "are you never together as a family?"

"Sure, but not here," said the kid through the door, "This is the outhouse!"

⌇

A man and woman were having dinner in a fine restaurant. They were gazing lovingly at each other and holding hands. Their waitress, taking another order at a table a few steps away suddenly noticed the man slowly sliding down his chair and under the table, but the woman acted unconcerned.

The waitress watched as the man slid all the way out down his chair out of sight under the table. Still, the woman appeared calm and unruffled; apparently unaware her dining companion had disappeared.

THE waitress went over to the table and said to the woman, "Pardon me, ma'am, but I think your husband just slid under the table."

The woman calmly looked up at her and said, "No, he didn't. He just walked in."

⤻

A man owned a small farm in Ireland. The Irish Internal Revenue determined he was not paying proper wages to his staff and sent an investigator out to interview him. "I need a list of your employees and how much you pay them," demanded the investigator.

"Well," replied the farmer, "There's my farmhand who's been here with me for three years. I pay him $200 a week plus free room and board. Then there's the cook who has been here for eighteen months, and I pay her $150 per week plus free room and board. Then there's the halfwit. He works about eighteen hours every day and does about ninety percent of the work around here. He makes about $10 a week. He pays his own room and board, and I buy him a bottle of whiskey every Saturday night. He also sleeps with my wife occasionally."

"That's the guy I want to talk to, the halfwit!" said the agent.

"That would be me," replied the farmer.

⤻

AN old Italian man is dying. He calls his grandson to his bedside, "Guido, I wan' you lissina me. I wan' you to take-a my chrome plated .38 revolver so you will always remember me."

"But grandpa, I really don't like guns. How about you leave me your Rolex watch instead?"

"You lissina me, boy. Somma day you gonna be runna da business, you gonna have a beautiful wife, lotsa money, a big-a home and maybe a couple of bambinos. Somma day you gonna come-a home and maybe finda you wife inna bed with another man. Whatta you gunna do then? Point to da watch and say, 'time's up'?"

Olof Swenson, out in his pasture in northern Minnesota, took a lightning quick kick from a cow—right in his crotch. Writhing in agony, he fell to the ground.

As soon as he could manage, he took himself to the doctor. He said, "How bad is it doc? I'm going on my honeymoon next veek and my fiancé, Lena, is still a virgin—in every vay."

The doctor told him, "Olaf, I'll have to put your willy in a splint to let it heal and keep it straight. It should be okay next week, but leave it on dere as long as you can." He took four tongue depressors and formed a neat little 4 sided splint, and taped it all together.

Olaf mentioned none of this to Lena, married her, and they went on their honeymoon to Duluth.

That night in the Holiday Inn, Lena ripped open her blouse to reveal her beautiful, untouched breasts. She said, "Olof, you're the first vun! No vun has EVER seen deez!"

Olof immediately dropped his pants and replied, "Look at dis Lena, still in da crate!"

⌒

A young Arab asks his father, What is this weird hat that we are wearing?

It is a "chechia" because in the desert it protects our heads from the sun!

And what is this type of clothing that we are wearing?

It's a "djbellah" because in the desert it is very hot and it protects your body!

And what are these ugly shoes that we have on our feet?

These are "babouches," which keep us from burning our feet when in the desert!

Tell me, papa...

Yes, my son?

Then, why are we living in Canada?

SAINT Peter is sitting at the Pearly Gates when two bandits arrive. He looked out through the gates and said, "Wait here, I will be right back."

St. Peter goes over to God's chambers and tells him who is waiting for entrance.

God says to Peter, "How many times do I have to tell you, you can't be racist and judgmental here. This is heaven, all are loved, and all are brothers. Go back and let them in!"

St. Peter goes back to the Gates, looks around, and lets out a heavy sigh. He returns to God's chambers and says, "Well, they're gone."

"Who, the bandits?" asked God

"No, the Pearly Gates."

EDDIE and Don, two friends, met in the park every day to feed the pigeons, watch the squirrels, and discuss world problems. One day Eddie didn't show up. Don didn't think much about it and figured maybe he had a cold or something. But after Eddie hadn't shown up for a week or so, Don got really worried. However, since the only time they ever got together was at the park, Don didn't know where Eddie lived, so he was unable to find out what had happened to him.

A month had passed, and Don figured he had seen the last of Eddie, but one day Don approached the park and lo and behold, there sat Eddie. Don was very excited and happy to see him and told him so, and then he said, "For crying out loud Eddie, what in the world happened to you?"

Eddie replied, "I have been in jail."

"Jail!" cried Don, "What in the world for?"

"Well," Eddie said, "you know Sue, that cute little blonde waitress at the coffee shop where I sometimes go?"

"Yeah," said Don, "I remember her, what about her?"

"Well, one day she filed rape charges against me; and at eighty-nine years old I was so proud that when I got into court, I pled guilty. The damn judge gave me thirty days for perjury."

Dave was staring sadly into his beer and sighed heavily.

"What's up Dave?" asked the bartender, "It's not like you to be so down in the mouth."

"It's my five year old son…" the man replied.

Don't tell me, he's in trouble for fighting in school? My lad's just the same—forget about it, it happens to boys that age," said the bartender sympathetically.

"I only wish it was that," continued the customer. "But it's far worse than that. The little jerk has got our gorgeous eighteen year old next door neighbor pregnant."

"Get away, that's impossible," gasped the bartender.

"It's not," said the man, "The little jerk stuck a pin in all my condoms."

⤳

PADDY was waiting at the bus stop with his mate when a lorry went by loaded up with rolls of turf. Paddy said, "I gonna do that when I win the lottery."

"What's dat?" says his mate.

"Send me lawn away to be cut."

⤳

TWO prostitutes were riding around town with a sign on top of their car which said, "Two Prostitutes, $50.00."

A policeman, seeing the sign, stopped them and told them they'd either have to remove the sign or go to jail.

Just at that time, another car passed with a sign saying, "Jesus Saves"

The prostitutes asked about the other car.

"Well that's a little different," the officer smiled, "their sign pertains to a religion."

The following day the same police officer noticed the same two hookers driving around with a large sign on their car. He figured he had an easy arrest until he read their new sign: "Two Fallen Angels, Seeking Peter – $50.00."

THE mother of a seventeen year old girl was concerned that her daughter was having sex. Worried the girl might become pregnant and adversely impact the family's status, she consulted the family doctor.

The doctor told her that teenagers today were very willful and any attempt to stop the girl would probably result in rebellion. He then told her to arrange for her daughter to be put on birth control and until then, talk to her and give her a box of condoms.

Later that evening, as he daughter was preparing for a date, the mother told her about the situation and handed her a box of condoms. The girl burst out laughing and reached over to hug her mother, saying, "Oh Mom! You don't have to worry about that, I'm dating Susan!"

⤸

A man went to church one day and afterward he stopped to shake the preacher's hand. He said, 'Preacher, I'll tell you, that was a damned fine sermon. Damned good!'

The preacher said, 'Thank you sir, but I'd rather you didn't use profanity.'

The man said, 'I was so damned impressed with that sermon I put five thousand dollars in the offering plate!'

The preacher said, 'No shit?'

⤸

BRENDA and Steve took their six-year-old son to the doctor. With some hesitation, they explained that although their little angel appeared to be in good health, they were concerned about his rather small penis. After examining the child, the doctor confidently declared, "Just feed him pancakes. That should solve the problem." The next morning when the boy arrived at breakfast, there was a large stack of warm pancakes in the middle of the table.

"Gee, Mom," he exclaimed, "for me?"

"Just take two," Brenda replied. "The rest are for your father."

ONE night, an eighty-seven year-old woman came home from Bingo to find her ninety-two year-old husband in bed with another woman. She became violent and ended up pushing him off the balcony of their twentieth floor apartment, killing him instantly. Brought before the court on the charge of murder, she was asked if she had anything to say in her own defense.

"Your Honor," she began coolly, "I figured that at ninety-two, if he could screw, he could fly."

⌒

A Doctor was addressing a large audience in Tampa. "The material we put into our stomachs is enough to have killed most of us sitting here, years ago. Red meat is awful. Soft drinks corrode your stomach lining. Chinese food is loaded with MSG. High fat diets can be disastrous, and none of us realizes the long-term harm caused by the germs in our drinking water. However, there is one thing that is the most dangerous of all and we all have eaten, or will eat it. Can anyone here tell me what food it is that causes the most grief and suffering for years after eating it?"

After several seconds of quiet, a seventy-five year-old man in the front row raised his hand, and softly said, "Wedding Cake."

⌒

BOB, a seventy year-old, extremely wealthy widower, shows up at the Country Club with a breathtakingly beautiful and very sexy twenty-five year-old blonde-haired woman who knocks everyone's socks off with her youthful sex appeal and charm and who hangs over Bob's arm and listens intently to his every word. His buddies at the club are all aghast.

At the very first chance, they corner him and ask, "Bob, how'd you get the trophy girlfriend?"

Bob replies, "Girlfriend? She's my wife!"

They are knocked over, but continue to ask. "So, how'd you persuade her to marry you?"

"I lied about my age," Bob replies.

"What, did you tell her you were only fifty?"

Bob smiles and says, "No, I told her I was ninety."

∽

Groups of Americans were travelling by tour bus through Holland. As they stopped at a cheese farm, a young guide led them through the process of cheese making, explaining that goat's milk was used. She showed the group a lovely hillside where many goats were grazing. "These," she explained, "are the older goats put out to pasture when they no longer produce." She then asked, "What do you do in America with your old goats?'"

A spry old gentleman answered, "They send us on bus tours!"

∽

A Sunday school teacher was telling her class the story of the Good Samaritan. She asked the class, "If you saw a person lying on the roadside, all wounded and bleeding, what would you do?" A thoughtful little girl broke the hushed silence, "I think I'd throw up."

∽

A Sunday school teacher asked, "Johnny, do you think Noah did a lot of fishing when he was on the Ark?" "No," replied Johnny. "How could he, with just two worms."

∽

A Sunday school teacher said to her children, "We have been learning how powerful kings and queens were in Bible times. But, there is a Higher Power. Can anybody tell me what it is?" One child blurted out, "Aces!"

A Sunday School teacher decided to have her young class memorize one of the most quoted passages in the Bible—Psalm 23. She gave the youngsters a month to learn the passage. Little Rick was excited about the task—but he just couldn't remember the Psalm. After much practice, he could barely get past the first line. On the day that the kids were scheduled to recite Psalm 23 in front of the congregation, Ricky was so nervous. When it was his turn, he stepped up to the microphone and said proudly, "The Lord is my Shepherd, and that's all I need to know."

THE preacher's five year-old daughter noticed that her father always paused and bowed his head for a moment before starting his sermon. One day, she asked him why. "Well, Honey," he began, proud that his daughter was so observant of his messages. "I'm asking the Lord to help me preach a good sermon." "How come he doesn't answer?" she asked.

A Rabbi said to a precocious six-year-old boy, "So your mother says your prayers for you each night? That's very commendable. What does she say?" The little boy replied, "Thank God he's in bed!"

WHEN my daughter, Kelli, said her bedtime prayers, she would bless every family member, every friend, and every animal (current and past). For several weeks, after we had finished the nightly prayer, Kelli would say, "And all girls." This soon became part of her nightly routine, to include this closing. My curiosity got the best of me and I asked her, "Kelli, why do you always add the part about all girls?" Her response, "Because everybody always finish their prayers by saying 'All Men'!"

Lᴵᴛᴛʟᴇ Johnny and his family were having Sunday dinner at his Grandmother's house. Everyone was seated around the table as the food was being served. When Little Johnny received his plate, he started eating right away.

"Johnny! Please wait until we say our prayer." said his mother.

"I don't need to," the boy replied.

"Of course, you do." his mother insisted. "We always say a prayer before eating at our house."

"That's at our house." Johnny explained. "But this is Grandma's house and she knows how to cook."

～

And They Ask: Why Do I Like Retirement?

Qᴜᴇsᴛɪᴏɴ: How many days in a week?
Aɴsᴡᴇʀ: 6 Saturdays, 1 Sunday

Qᴜᴇsᴛɪᴏɴ: When is a retiree's bedtime?
Aɴsᴡᴇʀ: Three hours after he falls asleep on the couch.

Qᴜᴇsᴛɪᴏɴ: How many retirees to change a light bulb?
Aɴsᴡᴇʀ: Only one, but it might take all day.

Qᴜᴇsᴛɪᴏɴ: What's the biggest gripe of retirees?
Aɴsᴡᴇʀ: There is not enough time to get everything done.

Qᴜᴇsᴛɪᴏɴ: Why don't retirees mind being called Seniors?
Aɴsᴡᴇʀ: The term comes with a 10% discount.

Qᴜᴇsᴛɪᴏɴ: Among retirees what is considered formal attire?
Aɴsᴡᴇʀ: Tied shoes.

Qᴜᴇsᴛɪᴏɴ: Why do retirees count pennies?
Aɴsᴡᴇʀ: They are the only ones who have the time.

QUESTION: What is the common term for someone who enjoys work and refuses to retire?

ANSWER: Nuts!

QUESTION: Why are retirees so slow to clean out the basement, attic or garage?

ANSWER: They know that as soon as they do, one of their adult kids will want to store stuff there.

QUESTION: What do retirees call a long lunch?

ANSWER: Normal.

QUESTION: What is the best way to describe retirement?

ANSWER: The never-ending coffee break.

QUESTION: What's the biggest advantage of going back to school as a retiree?

ANSWER: If you cut classes, no one calls your parents.

QUESTION: Why does a retiree often say he doesn't miss work, but misses the people he used to work with?

ANSWER: He is too polite to tell the whole truth.

And, my very favourite...

QUESTION: What do you do all week?

ANSWER: Monday through Friday, nothing... Saturday and Sunday, I rest.

Always remember this:

> You don't stop laughing because you grow old,
> You grow old because you stop laughing.

Did I Read It Right?

In a Washroom:
> TOILET OUT OF ORDER. PLEASE USE FLOOR BELOW

In a Laundromat:
> AUTOMATIC WASHING MACHINES:
> PLEASE REMOVE ALL YOUR CLOTHES
> WHEN THE LIGHT GOES OUT

In a Memphis department store:
> BARGAIN BASEMENT UPSTAIRS

In an office:
> WOULD THE PERSON WHO TOOK
> THE STEP LADDER YESTERDAY
> PLEASE BRING IT BACK
> OR FURTHER STEPS WILL BE TAKEN
>
> AFTER COFFEE BREAK
> STAFF SHOULD EMPTY THE COFFEE POT
> AND STAND UPSIDE DOWN ON THE DRAINING BOARD

Outside a second-hand shop:
> WE EXCHANGE ANYTHING
> —BICYCLES, WASHING MACHINES, ETC.
> WHY NOT BRING YOUR WIFE ALONG
> AND GET A WONDERFUL BARGAIN?

Notice in health food shop window:
> CLOSED DUE TO ILLNESS

Spotted in a safari park:
> ELEPHANTS PLEASE STAY IN YOUR CAR

Seen during a conference:
FOR ANYONE WHO HAS CHILDREN
AND DOESN'T KNOW IT,
THERE IS A DAY CARE ON THE FIRST FLOOR

Notice in a farmer's field:
THE FARMER ALLOWS WALKERS
TO CROSS THE FIELD FOR FREE,
BUT THE BULL CHARGES.

Message on a leaflet:
IF YOU CANNOT READ,
THIS LEAFLET WILL TELL YOU
HOW TO GET LESSONS

On a repair shop door:
WE CAN REPAIR ANYTHING.
(PLEASE KNOCK HARD ON THE DOOR
AS THE BELL DOESN'T WORK)

⌐

Sex With an Older Man

WHEN a famous man named George Burns was ninety-seven years old he was interviewed by a TV show host. She asked the man, "How do you carry so much energy with you? You are always working, and at your age I think that is remarkable."

George replied, "I just take good care of myself and enjoy what I do when I do it."

The lady said, "I understand you still do the sex thing, even at your age."

George said, "Of course I still do the sex thing, and I am quite good at it.

The lady said, I have never been with an older man. Would you do it with me?"

So they had sex and when they finished, she said, "I just don't believe I have ever been so satisfied. You are a remarkable man!"

George said, "The second time is even better than the first time."

She asked, "You can really do it again at your age?"

George said, "Just let me sleep for half an hour. You hold my testicles in your left hand and my penis in your right hand and wake me up in thirty minutes."

When she woke him up, they had great sex again, and the lady was beside herself with joy.

She said, "Oh George, I am astounded that you could do a repeat performance and have it be even better than the first time. At your age, Oh My, Oh My!"

George told her that the third time would be even better. "You just hold my testicles in your left hand and my penis in your right hand and call me in thirty minutes."

The lady asked, "Does my holding you like that kind of recharge your batteries?"

George replied, "No, but the last time I had sex with a woman like you. she stole my wallet!"

⌒

Airport Screening: Latest Statistics

Terrorists discovered: 0

Transvestites: 133

Hernias: 1,485

Hemorrhoid Cases: 3,172

Enlarge Prostates: 8,249

Breast Implants: 59,350

Natural Blondes: 3

A family doctor asked a pregnant prostitute in Come-by-Chance, Newfoundland... "Do you know who the father is?"

The prostitute replied "Lard Jasus By'e, when ya eats a tin of beans would ya know which one made you fart?!"

⌇

Angela Merkel arrives at Passport Control at Pair airport.

"Nationality?" asks the immigration officer

"German," she replies

"Occupation?"

"No, just here for a few days."

⌇

The police came to my front door last night holding a picture of me wife. They said, "Is this your wife, sir?"

Shocked, I answered, "Lard Jasus Yes by'e dats her."

They said, "I'm afraid it looks like she's been hit by a bus." I said, "I know by'e, but she's good to the kids and a good cook."

⌇

Jarge is in jail. The guard looks in his cell and sees him hanging by his feet. "What are you doing?" he asks.

"Hanging meself," Jarge replies.

"It should be round your neck," says the guard.

"I tried that," says Jarge from Krinkle Cove, "but I couldn't friggin' breathe."

The Wisdom of Larry the Cable Guy

EVERYONE concentrates on the problems we're having in our country lately: Illegal immigration, hurricane recovery, alligators attacking people in Florida…. Not me—I concentrate on solutions for the problems—it's a win-win situation. Dig a moat the length of the Mexican border. Send the dirt to New Orleans to raise the level of the levees. Put the Florida alligators in the moat along the Mexican border. Any other problems you would like for me to solve today?

Consider Cows, the Constitution, and the Ten Commandments:

- **Cows**: Is it just me, or does anyone else find it amazing that during the mad cow epidemic our government could track a single cow, born in Canada almost three years ago, right to the stall where she slept in the state of Washington? Furthermore they tracked her calves to their stalls. However they are unable to locate eleven million illegal aliens wandering around our country. Maybe we should give each of them a cow.
- **The Constitution**: They keep talking about drafting a Constitution for Iraq ….why don't we just give them ours? It was written by a lot of really smart guys, it has worked for over 200 years, and we're not using it anymore.
- **The 10 Commandments**: The real reason that we can't have the Ten Commandments posted in a courthouse is this — you cannot post 'Thou Shall Not Steal', 'Thou Shall Not Commit Adultery' and 'Thou Shall Not Lie' in a building full of lawyers, judges, and politicians, it creates a hostile work environment.

Also, think about this…if you don't want to forward this for fear of offending someone—you are part of the problem!

Get er done!

During my physical, my doctor asked me about my daily activity level, and so I described a typical day this way:

"Well, yesterday afternoon, I waded along the edge of a lake, drank eight beers, escaped from wild dogs in the heavy brush, marched up and down several rocky hills, stood in a patch of poison ivy, crawled out of quicksand, jumped away from an aggressive rattlesnake and took four 'leaks' behind big trees."

Inspired by the story, the doctor said, "You sound like one hell of an outdoorsman!"

"No," I replied, "I'm just a shitty golfer!"

⌒

A Canadian guy traveling in the US on vacation lost his wallet and all of his identification. Cutting his trip short, he attempted to make his way home but was stopped by the Canadian Customs Agent at the border.

"May I see your identification, please?" asked the agent.

"I'm sorry, but I lost my wallet," replied the guy.

"Sure buddy, I hear that one every day. No ID, no entry," said the agent.

"But I can prove I'm a Canadian!" he exclaimed. "I have a picture of Celine Dion tattooed on one butt cheek and Shania Twain on the other."

"This I got to see," replied the agent.

With that, the guy dropped his pants and showed the agent his behind.

"By golly, you're right!" exclaimed the agent. "Have a safe trip back to Ottawa."

"Thanks!" he said. "But how were you convinced I was from Canada?"

The agent replied, "I recognized your Prime Minister in the middle."

THE judge says to a double-homicide defendant, "You're charged with beating your wife to death with a hammer."

A voice at the back of the courtroom yells out, "You bastard!"

The judge says, "You're also charged with beating your mother-in-law to death with a hammer.±"

The voice in the back of the courtroom yells out, "You bastard!"

The judge stops and says to the guy in the back of the courtroom, "Sir, I can understand your anger and frustration at this crime. But no more outbursts from you, or I'll charge you with contempt. Is that understood?"

The guy in the back of the court stands up and says, "I'm sorry, Your Honour, but for fifteen years, I've lived next door to that bastard, and every time I asked to borrow a hammer, he said he didn't have one."

⌐

Wisdom in Phrases

"The cardiologist's diet: If it tastes good, spit it out."

"By all means, marry. If you get a good wife, you'll become happy; if you get a bad one, you'll become a philosopher."
— SOCRATES

"By the time a man is wise enough to watch his step, he's too old to go anywhere."
— BILLY CRYSTAL

"Don't worry about avoiding temptation. As you grow older, it will avoid you."
— WINSTON CHURCHILL

"I don't feel old. I don't feel anything until noon. Then it's time for my nap."
— BOB HOPE

"I had a rose named after me and I was very flattered. But I was not pleased to read the description in the catalogue: No good in a bed, but fine against a wall."

— ELEANOR ROOSEVELT

"I have never hated a man enough to give his diamonds back."

— ZSA ZSA GABOR

"I never drink water because of the disgusting things that fish do in it."

— W.C. FIELDS

"I was married by a judge. I should have asked for a jury."

— GROUCHO MARX

"Last week, I stated this woman was the ugliest woman I had ever seen. I have since been visited by her sister, and now wish to withdraw that statement."

— MARK TWAIN

"Maybe it's true that life begins at fifty… But everything else starts to wear out, fall out, or spread out."

— PHYLLIS DILLER

"Money can't buy you happiness…but it does bring you a more pleasant form of misery."

— SPIKE MILLIGAN

"My luck is so bad that if I bought a cemetery, people would stop dying."

— RODNEY DANGERFIELD

"My wife has a slight impediment in her speech. Every now and then she stops to breathe."

— JIMMY DURANTE

"Only Irish coffee provides in a single glass all four essential food groups: alcohol, caffeine, sugar, and fat."

— ALEX LEVINE

"Santa Claus has the right idea. Visit people only once a year."

— VICTOR BORGE

"Sometimes, when I look at my children, I say to myself, 'Lillian, you should have remained a virgin.'"

— LILLIAN CARTER [mother of Jimmy Carter]

"The secret of a good sermon is to have a good beginning and a good ending; and to have the two as close together as possible."

— GEORGE BURNS

"Until I was thirteen, I thought my name was SHUT UP."

— JOE NAMATH

"We could certainly slow the aging process down if it had to work its way through Congress."

— WILL ROGERS

⌐

Alcohol Labels Just Like Cigarettes

AMERICAN liquor manufacturers have accepted the FDA's suggestion that the following warning labels be placed immediately on all varieties of alcohol containers:

- **WARNING**: The consumption of alcohol may leave you wondering what the hell happened to your bra and panties.

- **WARNING**: The consumption of alcohol may make you think you are whispering when you are not.

- **WARNING**: The consumption of alcohol may cause you to tell your friends over and over again that you love them.

- **WARNING**: The consumption of alcohol may cause you to think you can sing.

- **WARNING**: The consumption of alcohol may lead you to believe that ex-lovers are really dying for you to telephone them at four in the morning.

- **WARNING**: The consumption of alcohol is the leading cause of inexplicable rug burns on the forehead, knees and lower back.

- **WARNING**: The consumption of alcohol may create the illusion that you are tougher, smarter, faster and better looking than most people.

- **WARNING**: The consumption of alcohol may lead you to think people are laughing WITH you.

- **WARNING**: The consumption of alcohol may cause pregnancy

- **WARNING**:The crumsumpten of alcahol may mack you tink you can tipe real gud.

∽

Dear Abby:

Dear Abby admitted she was at a loss to answer the foillowing:

Dear Abby:

A couple of women moved in across the hall from me. One is a middle-aged gym teacher and the other is a social worker in her mid-twenties. These two women go everywhere together and I've never seen a man go into or leave their apartment. Do you think they could be Lebanese?

Dear Abby:

What can I do about all the Sex, Nudity, Foul Language and Violence on my VCR?

Dear Abby:

I have a man I can't trust. He cheats so much, I'm not even sure the baby I'm carrying is his.

Dear Abby:

I am a twenty-three year old liberated woman who has been on the pill for two years. It's getting expensive and I think my boyfriend should share half the cost, but I don't know him well enough to discuss money with him.

Dear Abby:

I've suspected that my husband has been fooling around, and when confronted with the evidence, he denied everything and said it would never happen again.

Dear Abby:

Our son writes that he is taking Judo. Why would a boy who was raised in a good Christian home turn against his own?

Dear Abby:

I joined the Navy to see the world. I've seen it. Now how do I get out?

Dear Abby:

My forty year old son has been paying a psychiatrist five hundred dollars an hour every week for two and a half years. He must be crazy.

Dear Abby:

I was married to Bill for three months and I didn't know he drank until one night he came home sober.

Dear Abby:

My mother is mean and short tempered I think she is going through mental pause.

Dear Abby:

You told some woman whose husband had lost all interest in sex to send him to a doctor. Well, my husband lost all interest in sex and he is a doctor. Now what do I do?

Remember these people can vote!

⤳

A fifty-four year old woman had a heart attack and was taken to the hospital. While on the operating table she had a near death experience. Seeing God, she asked, "Is my time up?"

God said, "No, you have another forty-three years, two months, and eight days to live."

Upon recovery, the woman decided to stay in the hospital and have a face-lift, liposuction, breast implants, and a tummy tuck. She even had someone come in and change her hair colour and brighten her teeth. Since she had so much more time to live, she figured she might as well make the most of it.

After her last operation, she was released from the hospital. While crossing the street on her way home, she was killed by an ambulance.

Arriving in front of God, she demanded, "I thought you said I had another forty-three years?! Why didn't you pull me from out of the path of the ambulance?"

God replied: "Shit! I didn't recognize you."

THERE was a knock on the door this morning. I opened it to find a young man standing there who said: "Hello sir, I'm a Jehovah's Witness."

I said, "Come in and sit down."

I offered him coffee and asked, "What do you want to talk about?"

He said, "Beats the shit out of me, I've never gotten this far before."

⌒

THE boss walked into the office one morning not knowing his zipper was down and his fly area wide open.

His assistant walked up to him and said, "This morning when you left your house, did you close your garage door?"

The boss told her he knew he'd closed the garage door, and walked into his office puzzled by the question. As he finished his paperwork, he suddenly noticed his fly was open, and zipped it up. He then understood his assistant's question about his "garage door."

He headed out for a cup of coffee and paused by her desk to ask, "When my garage door was open, did you see my Hummer parked in there?"

She smiled and said, "No, I didn't. All I saw was an old minivan with two flat tires."

⌒

AN elderly gentleman had serious hearing problems for a number of years. He went to the doctor and the doctor was able to have him fitted for a set of hearing aids that allowed the gentleman to hear 100%.

The elderly gentleman went back in a month to the doctor and the doctor said, "Your hearing is perfect. Your family must be really pleased that you can hear again."

The gentleman replied, "Oh, I haven't told my family yet. I just sit around and listen to the conversations. I've changed my will three times!"

Two elderly gentlemen from a retirement center were sitting on a bench under a tree when one turns to the other and says:

"Slim, I'm eighty-three years old now and I'm just full of aches and pains. I know you're about my age. How do you feel?"

Slim says, "I feel just like a newborn baby."

"Really!? Like a newborn baby!?"

"Yep No hair, no teeth, and I think I just wet my pants."

An elderly couple had dinner at another couple's house and, after eating, the wives left the table and went into the kitchen. The two gentlemen were talking, and one said, "Last night we went out to a new restaurant and it was really great. I would recommend it very highly."

The other man said, "What is the name of the restaurant?"

The first man thought and thought and finally said, "What is the name of that flower you give to someone you love? You know…the one that's red and has thorns."

"Do you mean a rose?"

"Yes, that's the one," replied the man. He then turned towards the kitchen and yelled, "Rose, what's the name of that restaurant we went to last night?'

Hospital regulations require a wheel chair for patients being discharged. However, while working as a student nurse, I found one elderly gentleman already dressed and sitting on the bed with a suitcase at his feet, who insisted he didn't need my help to leave the hospital. After a chat about rules being rules, he reluctantly let me wheel him to the elevator.

On the way down I asked him if his wife was meeting him.

"I don't know," he said. "She's still upstairs in the bathroom changing out of her hospital gown."

A couple in their nineties is having problems remembering things. During a checkup, the doctor tells them that they're physically okay, but that they might want to start writing things down to help them remember.

Later that night, while watching TV, the old man gets up from his chair. "Want anything while I'm in the kitchen?" he asks.

"Will you get me a bowl of ice cream?"

"Sure…"

"Don't you think you should write it down so you can remember it?" she asks.

"No, I can remember it."

"Well, I'd like some strawberries on top, too. Maybe you should write it down, so as not to forget it?"

He says, "I can remember that. You want a bowl of ice cream with strawberries."

"I'd also like whipped cream. I'm certain you'll forget that, write it down?" she asks. Irritated, he says, "I don't need to write it down, I can remember it! Ice cream with strawberries and whipped cream—I got it, for goodness sake!"

Then he toddles into the kitchen. After about 20 minutes, the old man returns from the kitchen and hands his wife a plate of bacon and eggs…

She stares at the plate for a moment, then says "Where's my toast?"

⌣

A senior citizen said to his eighty-year old buddy: "So I hear you're getting married?"

"Yep!"

"Do I know her?"

"Nope!'"

"This woman, is she good looking?"

"Not really."

"Is she a good cook?"

"Naw, she can't cook too well."

"Does she have lots of money?"

"Nope! Poor as a church mouse."

"Well, then, is she good in bed?"

"I don't know."

"Well why in the world do you want to marry her then?"

"Because she can still drive!"

❧

Three old guys are out walking. First one says, "Windy, isn't it?" Second one says, "No, it's Thursday!"

Third one says, "So am I. Let's go get a beer…"

❧

A man was telling his neighbour, "I just bought a new hearing aid. It cost me four thousand dollars, but it's state of the art… It's perfect."

"Really," answered the neighbor. "What kind is it?"

'Twelve thirty."

❧

WILL, an eighty-two year-old man, went to the doctor to get a physical. A few days later, the doctor saw Will walking down the street with a gorgeous young woman on his arm. A couple of days later, the doctor spoke to Will and said, "You're really doing great, aren't you?"

Will replied, "Just doing what you said, Doc: 'Get a hot mamma and be cheerful.'"

The doctor said, "I didn't say that. I said: 'You've got a heart murmur; be careful.'"

A little old man shuffled slowly into an ice cream parlor and pulled himself slowly, painfully, up onto a stool. After catching his breath, he ordered a banana split.

The waitress asked kindly, "Crushed nuts?"

"No," he replied, "Arthritis."

                                    ⌒

A successful businessman was growing old and knew it was time to choose a successor to take over the business. Instead of choosing one of his Directors or his children, he decided to do something different. He called all the young executives in his company together. He said, "It is time for me to step down and choose the next CEO. I have decided to choose one of you."

The young executives were shocked, but the boss continued. "I am going to give each one of you a seed today—one very special seed. I want you to plant the seed, water it, and come back here one year from today with what you have grown from the seed I have given you. I will then judge the plants that you bring, and the one I choose will be the next CEO."

One man, named Jim, was there that day and he, like the others, received a seed. He went home and excitedly told his wife the story. She helped him get a pot, soil, and compost, and he planted the seed. Every day he would water it and watch to see if it had grown. After about three weeks, some of the other executives began to watch to see if it had grown. After about three weeks, some of the other executives began to talk about their seeds and the plants that were beginning to grow. Jim kept checking his seed, but nothing ever grew.

Three weeks, four weeks, five weeks went by, still nothing. By now, others were talking about their plants, but Jim didn't have a plant and he felt like a failure. Six months went by—still nothing in Jim's pot. He just knew he had killed his seed. Everyone else had trees and tall plants, but he had nothing. Jim didn't say anything to his colleagues, however he just kept watering and fertilizing the soil—he wanted the seed to grow. A year finally went by and all the young executives of the company brought their plants to the CEO for inspection.

Jim told his wife that he wasn't going to take an empty pot. But she asked him to be honest about what happened. Jim felt sick to his stomach, it was going to be the most embarrassing moment of his life, but he knew his wife was right. He took his empty pot to the boardroom. When Jim arrived, he was amazed at the variety of the plants grown by the other executives. They were beautiful—in all shapes and sizes. Jim put his empty pot on the floor and many of his colleagues laughed, a few felt sorry for him!

When the CEO arrived, he surveyed the room and greeted his young executives. Jim just tried to hide in the back. "My, what great plants, trees, and flowers you have grown," said the CEO. "Today one of you will be appointed the CEO!" All of a sudden, the CEO spotted Jim at the back of the room with his empty pot. He ordered the Financial Director to bring him to the front.

Jim was terrified. He thought, "The CEO knows I'm a failure! Maybe he will have me fired!"

When Jim got to the front, the CEO asked him what had happened to his seed. Jim told him the story. The CEO asked everyone to sit down except Jim. He looked at Jim, and then announced to the young executives, "Behold your next Chief Executive Officer!"

Jim couldn't believe it. Jim couldn't even grow his seed.

"How could he be the new CEO?" the others said.

Then the CEO said, "One year ago today, I gave everyone in this room a seed. I told you to take the seed, plant it, water it, and bring it back to me today. But I gave you boiled seeds; they were dead—it was not possible for them to grow. All of you, except Jim, brought me trees, and plants, and flowers. When you found that the seed would not grow, you substituted another seed for the one I gave you. Jim was the only one with the courage and honesty to bring me a pot with my seed in it. Therefore, he is the one who will be the new Chief Executive!"

- If you plant honesty, you will reap trust.
- If you plant goodness, you will reap friends.
- If you plant humility, you will reap greatness.
- If you plant perseverance, you will reap contentment.
- If you plant consideration, you will reap perspective.

- If you plant hard work, you will reap success.
- If you plant forgiveness, you will reap reconciliation.
- If you plant faith, you will reap a harvest.

So, be careful what you plant now; it will determine what you will reap later.

⌒

A road crew supervisor hired a nice-looking blonde woman to assist with painting the yellow line down the middle of the road. He was skeptical about hiring her, but she appeared enthusiastic and told him that she really needed the job. Her name was «Jo Jo». He explained to her that her work day would be to complete two miles of line on her road, and he set her up with her brushes and paint and got her started.

After the first day, he was pleased to find that she did an excellent job and was able to paint four miles of road in her eight-hour shift. He told her that she did an excellent job and how pleased he was with her progress.

On the second day, she completed painting two miles of road. Her supervisor was surprised that on day one she had completed twice as much work, but did not say anything, as two miles of road was the amount that the job required anyway. He decided to just accept it, and to look forward to the next day when he was sure that she would pick up her speed again.

On day three, he was shocked to learn that in her eight-hour shift, she only completed painting one mile of road. He called her into his office and asked her what was the problem.

"On your first day, you completed four miles of road, on your second day, two miles of road, and now on day three, you were only able to complete one mile of road. Can I ask you, what is the problem?»

"Well," she replied, "I'll tell you, but I thought you would know that every day I was getting farther and farther from the paint can."

THE madam opened the brothel door in Winnipeg and saw a rather dignified, well-dressed, good-looking man in his late forties or early fifties.

"May I help you sir?" she asked.

"I want to see Valerie," the man replied.

"Sir, Valerie is one of our most expensive ladies. Perhaps you would prefer someone else", said the madam.

"No, I must see Valerie," he replied.

Just then, Valerie appeared and announced to the man she charged $5,000 a visit. Without hesitation, the man pulled out five thousand dollars and gave it to Valerie, and they went upstairs. After an hour, the man calmly left. The next night, the man appeared again, once more demanding to see Valerie. Valerie explained that no one had ever come back two nights in a row, as she was too expensive. But there were no discounts. The price was still $5,000.

Again, the man pulled out the money, gave it to Valerie, and they went upstairs. After an hour, he left. The following night the man was there yet again. Everyone was astounded that he had come for a third consecutive night, but he paid Valerie and they went upstairs.

After their session, Valerie said to the man, "No one has ever been with me three nights in a row. Where are you from?"

The man replied, "Ontario."

"Really," she said. "I have family in Ontario."

"I know," the man said. "Your sister died, and I am her attorney. She asked me to give you your inheritance of $15,000."

The moral of the story is that three things in life are certain.

1. Death
2. Taxes
3. Being screwed by a lawyer

An attractive blonde from Cork, Ireland arrived at the casino. She seemed a little intoxicated and bet 20,000 Euros on a single roll of the dice. She said, "I hope you don't mind, but I feel much luckier when I'm completely nude." With that, she stripped from the neck down, rolled the dice and with an Irish brogue yelled, "Come on, baby, Mama needs new clothes!"

As the dice came to a stop, she jumped up and down and squealed, "Yes! Yes! I won, I Won!" She hugged each of the dealers and then picked up her winnings and her clothes and quickly departed.

The dealers stared at each other dumbfounded. Finally, one of them asked, "What did she roll?" The other answered, "I don't know. I thought you were watching."

The morals of this story are:

1. Not all Irish are drunks.
2. Not all blondes are dumb.
3. But all men…are men.

⌒

Two women were sitting next to each other at a bar. After a while one looks at the other and says, "I can't help but think, from listening to you, that you're from Ireland. The other woman responds proudly, "Yes, I sure am!"

The first one says, "So am I! Whereabouts in Ireland are ya from?"

The other woman answers, "I'm from St. John's, I am."

The first one responds, "So, am I! And what street did you live on?"

The other woman says, "A lovely little area it was in the west end. I lived on Warbury Street in the old central part of town."

The first one says, "Faith and it's a small world. So did I! And what school did ya go to?"

The other woman answers, "Well now, I went to Holy Heart of Mary, of course."

The first one gets really excited and says, "And so did I. Tell me, what year did you graduate?"

The other woman answers, "Well, now, let's see. I graduated in 1964."

The first woman exclaims, "The Good Lord must be smiling down upon us! I can hardly believe our good luck at winding up in the same pub tonight. Can you believe it? I graduated from Holy Heart of Mary in 1964 me self."

About this time, a man walks into the bar, sits down and orders a beer. Brian, the bartender, walks over to him, shaking his head and muttering, "It's going to be a long night tonight."

The man gives him a quizzical look, "Why do you say that?"

The bartender explains, "The Murphy twins are drunk again."

⌐

ABORIGINAL tracker somewhere between Karratha and Onslow in Western Australia.

An Australian tour guide was showing a group of American tourists the Top End. On their way to Kakadu, he was describing the abilities of the Australian Aborigine to track man or beast over land, through the air, under the sea. The Americans were incredulous. Later in the day, the tour rounded a bend on the highway and discovered, lying in the middle of the road, an Aborigine. He had one ear pressed to the white line whilst his left leg was held high in the air. The tour stopped and the guide and the tourists gathered around the prostrate Aborigine.

"Jacky," said the tour guide, "what are you tracking and what are you listening for?"

The aborigine replied, "Down the road about twenty-five miles is a 1971 Baliant Ute. It's a red one. The left front tire is bald. The front end is out of whack, and him got bloody dents in every panel. There are nine black fellas in the back, all drinking warm sherry. There are three kangaroos on the roof rack and six dogs on the front seat."

The American tourists moved forward, astounded by this precise and detailed knowledge. "God man, how do you know all that?" asked one.

The Aborigine replied "I fell out off the pucken thing about half an hour ago!"

THREE women and three men are travelling by train to the football game. At the station, the three men each buy a ticket and watch as the three women buy just one ticket.

"How are the three of you going to travel on only one ticket?" asks one of the men.

"Watch and learn," answers one of the women.

They all board the train. The three men take their respective seats but all three women cram into a toilet together and close the door. Shortly after the train has departed, the conductor comes around collecting tickets. He knocks on the toilet door and says, "Ticket, please." The door opens just a crack, and a single arm emerges with a ticket in hand. The conductor takes it and moves on.

The men see this happen and agree it was quite a clever idea; so, after the game, they decide to do the same thing on the return trip and save some money. When they get to the station they buy a single ticket for the return trip but see, to their astonishment, that the three women don't buy any ticket at all!

"How are you going go to travel without a ticket?" says one perplexed man.

"Watch and learn," answer the women.

When they board the train, the three men cram themselves into a toilet, and the three women cram into another toilet just down the way. Shortly after the train is on its way, one of the women leaves her toilet and walks over to the toilet in which the men are hiding.

The woman knocks on their door and says, "Ticket, please."

I'm still trying to figure out why men ever think they are smarter than women.

⤳

YESTERDAY I had an appointment to see the urologist for a prostate exam. Of course I was a bit on edge because all my friends have either gone under the knife or had those pellets implanted. The waiting room was filled with patients. As I approached the receptionist's desk, I noticed that the receptionist was a large unfriendly woman who looked like a Sumo wrestler. I gave her my name.

In a very loud voice, the receptionist said, "Yes, I have your name here; you want to see the doctor about impotence, right?"

All the patients in the waiting room snapped their heads around to look at me, a now very embarrassed man.

But as usual, I recovered quickly, and in an equally loud voice replied, "No, I've come to inquire about a sex change operation, but I don't want the same doctor that did yours."

∽

A woman was at her hairdresser's getting her hair styled for a trip to Rome with her husband. She mentioned the trip to the hairdresser, who responded, "Rome? Why would anyone want to go there? It's crowded and dirty. You're crazy to go to Rome. So, how are you getting there?"

"We're taking Continental," was the reply. "We got a great rate!"

"Continental?" exclaimed the hairdresser. "That's a terrible airline. Their planes are old, their flight attendants are ugly, and they're always late. So, where are you staying in Rome?"

"We'll be at an exclusive little place over on Rome's Tiber River called Teste."

"Don't go any further. I know that place. Everybody thinks it's gonna be something special and exclusive, but it's really a dump, the worst hotel in the city! The rooms are small, the service is surly, and they're overpriced. So, whatcha' doing when you get there?"

"We're going to go to see the Vatican and we hope to see the Pope."

"That's rich," laughed the hairdresser. "You and a million other people trying to see him. He'll look the size of an ant. Boy, good luck on this lousy trip of yours. You're going to need it."

A month later, the woman again came in for a hairdo. The hairdresser asked her about her trip to Rome.

"It was wonderful," explained the woman. "Not only were we on time in one of Continental's brand new planes, but it was overbooked and they bumped us up to first class. The food and wine were wonderful, and I had a handsome twenty-eight year-old steward who waited on me hand and foot. And the hotel was great! They'd just finished a five million dollar remodeling job and now it's a jewel, the finest hotel in the city. They, too, were overbooked, so they apologized and gave us their owner's suite at no extra charge!"

"Well," muttered the hairdresser, "that's all well and good, but I know you didn't get to see the Pope."

"Actually, we were quite lucky, because as we toured the Vatican, a Swiss Guard tapped me on the shoulder, and explained that the Pope likes to meet some of the visitors, and if I'd be so kind as to step into his private room and wait, the Pope would personally greet me. Sure enough, five minutes later, the Pope walked through the door and shook my hand! I knelt down and he spoke a few words to me."

"Oh, really! What'd he say?"

"He said, 'Where did you get that lousy hairdo?'"

⌐

A husband and wife are on the ninth green when suddenly she collapses from a heart attack!

"Help me dear," she groans to her husband.

The husband calls 911 on his cell phone, talks for a minute, picks up his putter and lines up his putt.

His wife raises her head off the green and stares at him.

"I'm dying here and you're putting?"

"Don't worry dear," says the husband calmly, "they found a doctor on the second hole and he's coming to help you.

"Well, how long will it take for him to get here?" she asks feebly.

"No time at all," says her husband. "Everybody's already agreed to let him play through."

⌐

A reporter told Phil Mickelson, "You are spectacular. Your name is synonymous with the game of golf. You really know your way around the course. What's your secret?"

Mickelson replied, "The holes are numbered."

A young man and a priest are playing golf together.
"This next hole is a short Par-3," says the Priest. "What are you going to use on this hole, my son?"

The young man says, "An 8-iron, Father. What about you?"

The priest says, "I'm going to hit a soft seven and pray."

The young man hits his 8-iron and puts the ball on the green.

The Priest tops his 7-iron and dribbles the ball out a few yards.

The young man says, "I don't know about you, Father, but in my church, when we pray, we keep our heads down."

⌒

POLICE were called to an apartment and find a woman holding a bloody 5-iron standing over a lifeless man.

The detective asks, "Ma'am, is that your husband?"

"Yes," says the woman.

"Did you hit him with that golf club?"

"Yes, yes, I did." The woman begins to sob, drops the club, and puts her hands on her face.

"How many times did you hit him?"

"I don't know—five, six, maybe seven times—but just put me down for a five."

⌒

A golfer teed up his ball on the first tee, took a mighty swing and hit his ball into a clump of trees. He found it and saw an opening between two trees he thought he could hit through. Taking out his 3-wood, he took a mighty swing. The ball hit a tree, bounced back, hit him in the forehead and killed him.

As he approached the gates of Heaven, St. Peter asked, "Are you a good golfer?"

The man replied: "Got here in two, didn't I?"

THE bride was escorted down the aisle. When she reached the altar, the groom was standing there with his golf bag and clubs at his side.

She said: "What are your golf clubs doing here?"

He looked her right in the eye and said, "This isn't going to take all day, is it?"

⌒

Two rednecks, Larry and Doug, are sitting at their favourite bar, drinking beer.

Larry turns to Doug and says, "You know, I'm tired of going through life without an education. Tomorrow I think I'll go to the Community College and sign up for some classes."

Doug agrees it's a good idea and the two leave. The next day, Larry goes down to the college and meets the Dean of Admissions, who signs him up for the four basic classes: Math, English, History, and Logic.

"Logic?" Larry says. "What's that?"

The Dean says, "I'll give you an example. Do you own a weed eater?"

"Yeah."

"Then logically speaking, because you own a weed eater, I think that you would have a yard."

"That's true, I do have a yard."

"Because you have a yard, I think logically that you would have a house."

"Yes, I do have a house."

"And because you have a house, I think that you might logically have a family."

"Yes, I have a family!"

"I'm not done yet. Because you have a family, then logically you have a wife. And because you have a wife, then logic tells me you must be a heterosexual."

"I am a heterosexual! That's amazing; you were able to find out all of that because I have a weed eater."

Excited to take the class now, Larry shakes the Dean's hand and leaves to go meet Doug at the bar. He tells Doug about his classes, how he is signed up for Math, English, History, and Logic.

"Logic?" Doug says, "What's that?"

Larry says, "I'll give you an example. Do you have a weed eater?"

"No."

"Then you're homosexual!"

Up!

I'M sure you will enjoy this. I never knew one word in the English language that can be a noun, verb, adjective, adverb, and preposition.

This two-letter word in English has more meanings than any other two-letter word, and that word is "UP." It is listed in the dictionary as an [adv], [prep], [adj], [n] or [v]. It's easy to understand UP, meaning toward the sky or at the top of the list, but when we awaken in the morning, why do we wake UP?

At a meeting, why does a topic come UP? Why do we speak UP, and why are the officers UP for election and why is it UP to the secretary to write UP a report? We call UP our friends, brighten UP a room, polish UP the silver, warm UP the leftovers and clean UP the kitchen. We lock UP the house and fix UP the old car.

At other times, this little word has real special meaning. People stir UP trouble, line UP for tickets, work UP an appetite, and think UPexcuses.

To be dressed is one thing but to be dressed UP is special.

And this UP is confusing: A drain must be opened UP because it is stopped UP. We open UP a store in the morning but we close it UP at night. We seem to be pretty mixed UP about UP! To be knowledgeable about the proper uses of UP, look UP the word UP in the dictionary. In a desk-sized dictionary, it takes UP almost a quarter of the page and can add UP to about thirty definitions.

If you are UP to it, you might try building UP a list of the many ways UP is used. It will take UP a lot of your time, but if you don't give UP, you may wind UP with a hundred or more.

When it threatens to rain, we say it is clouding UP. When the sun comes out, we say it is clearing UP. When it rains, it soaks UP the earth. When it does not rain for a while, things dry UP. One could go on and on, but I'll wrap it UP, for now...my time is UP!

Oh...one more thing: What is the first thing you do in the morning and the last thing you do at night?

U

P!

⌐

Wife: "What are you doing?"
Husband: "Nothing."
Wife: "Nothing...? You've been reading our marriage certificate for an **hour.**"
Husband: "I was looking for the expiration date."

⌐

Wife: "Do you want dinner?"
Husband: "Sure! What are my choices?"
Wife: "Yes or no."

⌐

Girl: "When we get married, I want to share all your worries, troubles, and lighten your burden."
Boy: "When we get married, I want to share all your worries, troubles, and lighten your burden."
Girl: "Well that's because we aren't married yet."

Son: "Mum, when I was on the bus with Dad this morning, he told me to give up my seat to a lady."

Mom: "Well, you have done the right thing."

Son: "But Mum, I was sitting on Daddy's lap."

꒱

A newly married man asked his wife, "Would you have married me if my father hadn't left me a fortune?"

"Honey," the woman replied sweetly, "I'd have married you, no matter who left you a fortune!"

꒱

A wife asked her husband: "What do you like most in me, my pretty face or my sexy body?"

He looked at her from head to toe and replied: "I like your sense of humour!"

꒱

A man was sitting reading his papers when his wife hit him round the head with a frying pan.

"What was that for?" the man asked.

The wife replied, "That was for the piece of paper with the name Jenny on it that I found in your pants pocket."

The man then said. "When I was at the races last week Jenny was the name of the horse I bet on."

The wife apologized and went on with the housework. Three days later the man is watching TV when his wife bashes him on the head with an even bigger frying pan, knocking him unconscious.

Upon re-gaining consciousness the man asked why she had hit again.

The wife replied, "Your horse phoned."

Born 1930 – 1979

FIRST, we survived being born to mothers who smoked and/or drank while they carried us. They took aspirin, ate blue cheese dressing and didn't get tested for diabetes.

Then after that trauma, our baby cribs were covered with bright colored lead-based paints.

We had no childproof lids on medicine bottles, doors, or cabinets and when we rode our bikes, we had no helmets, not to mention the risks we took hitchhiking.

As children, we would ride in cars with no seat belts or air bags. Riding in the back of a pick-up on a warm day was always a special treat.

We drank water from the garden hose and not from a bottle. We shared one soft drink with four friends, from one bottle and on one actually died from this.

We ate cupcakes, bread and butter, and drank soda pop with sugar in it, but we weren't overweight because we were always outside playing.

We would leave home in the morning and play all day, as long as we were back when the streetlights came on.

No one was able to reach us all day. And we were okay. We would spend hours building our go-carts out of scraps and then ride down the hill, only to find out we had forgotten the brakes. After running into the bushes a few times, we learned to solve the problem.

We did not have Playstations, Nintendo's, X-boxes, no video games at all, no 99 channels on cable, no videotape movies, no surround sound, no cell phones, no personal computers, no Internet or Internet chat rooms...we had friends and we went outside and found them!

We fell out of trees, got cut, broke bones and teeth and there were no lawsuits from these accidents.

We made up games with sticks and tennis balls and ate worms; and although we were told it would happen, we did not put out very many eyes, nor did the worms live in us forever.

We rode bikes or walked to a friend's house and knocked on the door or rang the bell, or just walked in and talked to them!

Little League had tryouts and not everyone made the team. Those who didn't had to learn to deal with disappointment. Imagine that!

The idea of a parent bailing us out if we broke the law was unheard of. They actually sided with the law!

This generation has produced some of the best ever risk-takers, problem solvers, and inventors!

The past 50 years have seen an explosion of innovation and new ideas.

We had freedom, failure, success, and responsibility, and we learned how to deal with it all!

And you are one of them! Congratulations!

⌐

THERE was a bit of confusion at the store this morning. When I was ready to pay for my groceries, the cashier said, "Strip down facing me."

Making a mental note to complain to my congressman about Homeland Security running amok, I did just as she had instructed.

When the hysterical shrieking and alarms finally subsided, I found out that she was referring to my credit card.

I have been asked to shop elsewhere in the future.

They need to make their instructions to us seniors a little clearer!

⌐

A Spanish teacher was explaining to her class that in Spanish, unlike English, nouns are designated as either masculine or feminine. "House" for instance, is feminine: "la casa." "Pencil," however, is masculine: "el lapiz."

A student asked, "What gender is "computer?"

Instead of giving the answer, the teacher split the class into two groups, male and female, and asked them to decide for themselves whether "computer" should be a masculine or a feminine noun. Each group was asked to give four reasons for its recommendation.

The men's group decided that "computer" should definitely be of the feminine gender ("a computadora"), because:

1. No one but their creator understands their internal logic;
2. The native language they use to communicate with other computers is incomprehensible to everyone else;
3. Even the smallest mistakes are stored in long term memory for possible later retrieval; and
4. As soon as you make a commitment to one, you find yourself spending half your paycheck on accessories for it.

The women's group, however, concluded that computers should be Masculine ("el computador"), because:

1. In order to do anything with them, you have to turn them on;
2. They have a lot of data but still can't think for themselves;
3. They are supposed to help you solve problems, but half the time they ARE the problem; and
4. As soon as you commit to one, you realize that if you had waited a little longer, you could have gotten a better model.

The women won!

~

OUR teacher asked us what our favourite animal was, and I said, "Fried chicken."

She said I wasn't funny, but she couldn't have been right, since everyone else in the class laughed. My parents told me to always be truthful and honest, and I am. Fried chicken is my favourite animal. I told my dad what happened, and he said my teacher was probably a member of PETA. He said they love animals very much.

I do, too. Especially chicken, pork, and beef. Anyway, my teacher sent me to the principal's office. I told him what happened, and he laughed too. Then he told me not to do it again. The next day in class my teacher asked me what my favorite live animal was. I told her it was chicken.

She asked me why, just like she'd asked the other children. So I told her it was because you could make them into fried chicken. She sent me back to the principal's office again. He laughed, and told me not to do it again.

I don't understand. My parents taught me to be honest, but my teacher doesn't like it when I am. Today, my teacher asked us to tell her what famous person we admire most.

I told her, "Colonel Sanders." Guess where I am now...

⌁

Two lawyers had been stranded on a desert island for several months. The only thing on the island was a tall coconut tree that provided them their only food. Each day one of the lawyers would climb to the top to see if he could spot a rescue boat coming.

One day the lawyer yelled down from the tree, "Wow, I just can't believe my eyes. There is a woman out there floating in our direction."

The lawyer on the ground was most skeptical and said, "You're hallucinating; you've finally lost your mind."

But within a few minutes, up to the beach floated a stunningly beautiful woman, face up, totally naked, unconscious, without even so much as a ring or earrings on her person.

The two lawyers went down to the water, dragged her up on the beach and discovered, yes, she was alive, warm, conscious, and breathing.

One said to the other, "You know, we've been on this God-forsaken island for months now without a woman. It's been such a long, long time, so do you think we should...well...you know...screw her?"

"Out of what?," asked the other.

The Great Aussie Love Poem

Of course I love ya darling, you're a bloody top-notch bird
And when I say you're gorgeous, I mean every single word
So ya bum is on the big side, I don't mind a bit of flab
It means that when I'm ready, there's something' there to grab
So your belly isn't flat no more, I tell ya, I don't care
So long as when I cuddle ya, I can get my arms round there
No Sheila who is your age has nice round perky breasts
They just gave into gravity, but I know ya did ya best
I'm tellin' ya the truth now, I never tell ya lies
I think it's very sexy that you've got dimples on ya thighs
I swear upon me Nanna's grave, the moment that we met
I thought u was as good as I was ever gonna get
No matter wot u look like, I'll always love ya dear
Now shut up while the footys on, and get me bloody beer!

⌒

ONE winter morning a husband and wife in Northern Colorado were listening to the radio during breakfast. They heard the announcer say, "We're going to have eight to ten inches of snow today. You must park your car on the even-numbered side of the street, so the snow-ploughs can get through." So the good wife went out and moved her car.

A week later while they were having breakfast again, the radio announcer said, "We're expecting ten to twelve inches of snow today. You must park your car on the odd-numbered side of the street, so the snow-ploughs can get through." The good wife went out and moved her car again.

The next week they are again having breakfast, when the radio announcer says, "We're expecting twelve to fourteen inches of snow today and... ."

Just then the electricity went off.

The wife had a worried look on her face when she said, "Honey, I don't know what to do. Which side of the street do I need to park on so the snow-ploughs can get through?"

With love and understanding in his voice—that all men who are married to blondes exhibit—the husband replied, "Why don't you just leave it in the garage this time?"

⌒

I was a very happy person. My wonderful girlfriend and I had been dating for over a year, and so we decided to get married. There was only one little thing bothering me…it was her beautiful younger sister. My prospective sister-in-law was twenty-two, wore very tight miniskirts, and generally went around braless. She would regularly bend down when she was near me, and I always got more than a pleasant view of her private parts. It had to be deliberate. She never did it when she was near anyone else.

One day, little sister called and asked me to come over to check the wedding invitations. She was alone when I arrived, and she whispered to me that she had feelings and desires for me that she couldn't overcome. She told me that she wanted to make love to me just once before I got married and committed my life to her sister. Well, I was in total shock, and couldn't say a word.

She said, I'm going upstairs to my bedroom, and if you want one last wild fling, just come up and get me. I was stunned and frozen in shock as I watched her go up the stairs. When she reached the top she pulled off her panties and threw them down the stairs at me.

I stood there for a moment, then turned and made a beeline straight to the front door. I opened the door, and headed straight towards my car. Lo and behold, my entire future family was standing outside, all clapping!

With tears in his eyes, my father-in-law hugged me and said, we are very happy that you have passed our little test…we couldn't ask for better man for our daughter. Welcome to the family. And the moral of this story is: Always keep your condoms in your car!

Fifteen Reasons You Don't Take Your Man Shopping

AFTER I retired, my wife insisted that I accompany her on her trips to Target. Unfortunately, like most men, I found shopping boring and preferred to get in and get out. Equally unfortunate, my wife is like most women—she loves to browse. Yesterday my dear wife received the following letter from the local Target.

Dear Mrs. Samuel:

Over the past six months, your husband has caused quite a commotion in our store. We cannot tolerate this behaviour and have been forced to ban both of you from the store. Our complaints against your husband, Mr. Samuel, are listed below and are documented by our video surveillance cameras.

1. **June 15**: Took 24 boxes of condoms and randomly put them in other people's carts when they weren't looking.
2. **July 2**: Set all the alarm clocks in Housewares to go off at 5-minute intervals.
3. **July 7**: He made a trail of tomato juice on the floor leading to the women's restroom.
4. **July 19**: Walked up to an employee and told her in an official voice, "Code 3 in Housewares. Get on it right away." This caused the employee to leave her assigned station and receive a reprimand from her Supervisor that in turn resulted in a union grievance, causing management to lose time and costing the company money.
5. **August 4**: Went to the Service Desk and tried to put a bag of M&Ms on layaway.
6. **August 14**: Moved a "CAUTION—WET FLOOR" sign to a carpeted area.
7. **August 15**: Set up a tent in the camping department and told the children shoppers he'd invite them in if they would bring pillows and blankets from the bedding department to which twenty children obliged.

8. **August 23**: When a clerk asked if they could help him he began crying and screamed, "Why can't you people just leave me alone?" EMTs were called.

9. **September 4**: Looked right into the security camera and used it as a mirror while he picked his nose.

10. **September 10**: While handling guns in the hunting department, he asked the clerk where the antidepressants were.

11. **October 3**: Darted around the store suspiciously while loudly humming the "Mission Impossible" theme.

12. **October 6**: In the auto department, he practiced his "Madonna look" by using different sizes of funnels.

13. **October 18**: Hid in a clothing rack and when people browsed through, yelled "Pick me. Pick me!"

14. **October 21**: When an announcement came over the loud speaker, he assumed a fetal position and screamed "Oh no! It's those voices again!"

15. **October 23**: Went into a fitting room, shut the door, waited awhile, then yelled very loudly, "Hey! There's no toilet paper in here." One of the clerks passed out.

⌒

KING Ozymandias of Assyria was running low on cash after years of war with the Hittites. His last great possession was the Star of the Euphrates, the most valuable diamond in the ancient world. Desperate, he went to Croesus, the pawnbroker, to ask for a loan.

Croesus said, "I'll give you 100,000 dinars for it."

"But I paid a million dinars for it," the King protested. "Don't you know who I am? I am the king!"

Croesus replied, "When you wish to pawn a Star, makes no difference who you are."

EVIDENCE has been found that William Tell and his family were avid bowlers. Unfortunately, all the Swiss league records were destroyed in a fire…and so we'll never know for whom the Tells bowled.

⤝

A man rushed into a busy doctor's office and shouted, "Doctor! I think I'm shrinking!" The doctor calmly responded, "Now, settle down. You'll just have to be a little patient."

⤝

A marine biologist developed a race of genetically engineered dolphins that could live forever if they were fed a steady diet of seagulls. One day, his supply of the birds ran out so he had to go out and trap some more. On the way back, he spied two lions asleep on the road. Afraid to wake them, he gingerly stepped over them. Immediately, he was arrested and charged with transporting gulls across sedate lions for immortal porpoises.

⤝

BACK in the 1800's the Tate's Watch Company of Massachusetts wanted to produce other products, and since they already made the cases for watches, they used them to produce compasses. The new compasses were so bad that people often ended up in Canada or Mexico rather than California. This, of course, is the origin of the expression: …He who has a Tate's is lost!"

⤝

A thief broke into the local police station and stole all the toilets and urinals, leaving no clues. A spokesperson was quoted as saying, "We have absolutely nothing to go on."

An Indian chief was feeling very sick, so he summoned the medicine man. After a brief examination, the medicine man took out a long, thin strip of elk rawhide and gave it to the chief, telling him to bite off, chew, and swallow one inch of the leather every day. After a month, the medicine man returned to see how the chief was feeling. The chief shrugged and said, "The thong is ended, but the malady lingers on."

A famous Viking explorer returned home from a voyage and found his name missing from the town register. His wife insisted on complaining to the local civic official who apologized profusely saying, "I must have taken Leif off my census."

There were three Indian squaws. One slept on a deer hide, one slept on an elk hise, and the third slept on a hippopotamus hide. All three became pregnant. The first two each had a baby boy. The one who slept on the hippopotamus hide had twin boys. This just goes to prove that: "the squaw of the hippopotamus is equal to the sons of the squaws of the other two hides."

A skeptical anthropologist was cataloguing South American folk remedies with the assistance of a tribal Brujo who indicated that the leaves of a particular fern were a sure cure for any case of constipation. When the anthropologist expressed his doubts, the Brujo looked him in the eye and said, "Let me tell you, with fronds like these, you don't need enemas."

A woman goes to the doctor in England, worried about her husband's temper and threatening manner.

The doctor asks: "What's the problem, Janet?"

The woman says: "Well Doctor Cameron, I don't know what to do. Every time my husband comes home drunk, he threatens to slap me around."

The Doctor says: "Yes, well, I have a real good cure for that. When your husband arrives home intoxicated, just take a small glass of water and start to swish it around in your mouth. Just swish and swish but don't swallow it until he goes to bed and is sound asleep."

Two weeks later she comes back to the doctor looking fresh and reborn. She says: "Doctor that was brilliant! Every time my hubbie came home drunk, I swished with water. I swished and swished, and he didn't touch me even once! Tell me Doctor Cameron what's the secret? How's the water do that?"

The Doctor says: "Janet, it's really no big secret. The water does bugger all—it's keeping your mouth shut that does the trick!"

~

How NOT to Become a Millionaire

NEW YORK: Idaho resident Kathy Evans brought humiliation to her friends and family Tuesday when she set a new standard for stupidity with her appearance on the popular TV show, "Who Wants To Be A Millionaire." It seems that Evans, a 32-year-old wife and mother of two, got stuck on the first question, and proceeded to make what fans of the show are dubbing "the absolute worst use of lifelines ever." After being introduced to the show's host Meredith Vieira, Evans assured her that she was ready to play, whereupon she was posed with an extremely easy one hundred dollar question. The question was:

"Which of the following is the largest?"

a. A Peanut
b. An Elephant
c. The Moon
d. Hey, who you calling large?

Immediately Mrs. Evans was struck with an all-consuming panic as she realized that this was a question to which she did not readily know the answer. "Hmm, oh boy, that's a toughie," said Evans, as Vieira did her level best to hide her disbelief and disgust. "I mean, I'm sure I've heard of some of these things before, but I have no idea how large they would be."

Evans made the decision to use the first of her three lifelines, the 50/50.

Answers A and D were removed, leaving her to decide which was bigger, an elephant or the moon. However, faced with an incredibly easy question, Evans still remained unsure.

"Oh! It removed the two I was leaning towards!" exclaimed Evans. "Darn. I think I better phone a friend," in doing so using the second of her two lifelines on the first question. Mrs. Evans asked to be connected with her friend Betsy, who is an office assistant.

"Hi Betsy! How are you? This is Kathy! I'm on TV!" said Evans, wasting the first seven seconds of her call.

"Okay, I got an important question. Which of the following is the largest? B. an elephant, or C. the moon. Fifteen seconds hun."

Betsy quickly replied that the answer was C, the moon.

Evans proceeded to argue with her friend for the remaining ten seconds. "Come on Betsy, are you sure?" said Evans. [How sure are you? Puh, that can't be it." To everyone's astonishment, the moronic Evans declined to take her friend's advice and picked "The Moon."

"I just don't know if I can trust Betsy. She's not all that bright. So I think I'd like to ask the audience,' said Evans. Asked to vote on the correct answer, the audience returned ninety-eight percent in favour of answer C. "The Moon."

Having used up all her lifelines, Evans then made the dumbest choice of her life.

"Wow, seems like everybody is against what I'm thinking," said the too-stupid-to-live Evans. "But you know, sometimes you just got to go with your gut. So, let's see. For which is larger, an elephant or the moon, I'm going to have to go with B, an elephant. As my final answer."

Evans sat before the dumbfounded audience, the only one waiting with bated breath, and was told that she was wrong, and that the answer was in fact, C. "The Moon."

⤻

M AN driving down road, woman driving up the same road. They pass each other.
Woman yells out window, Pig!
Man yells out window, Jerk!
Man rounds the next curve.
Man crashes into a huge pig in middle of the road and dies.

Thought for the day: If man would just listen.

⤻

A young cowboy from Southern Alberta goes off to University. Half way through the semester, having foolishly squandered all his money, he calls home.

"Dad," he says, "You won't believe what modern education is developing! They actually have a program here at the University that will teach our dog, Ole' Blue how to talk!"

"That's amazing," his Dad says. "How do I get Ole' Blue into that program?"

"Just send him here with $1,000," the young cowboy says, "and I'll get him registered in the course."

So, his father sends the dog and $1,000. About two-thirds of the way through the semester, the money again runs out. The boy calls home.

"So how's Ole' Blue doing son?" his father asks.

"Awesome, Dad, he's talking up a storm," he says, "but you just won't believe this, they've had such good results with the talking that they have started to teach the animals how to read!"

"Read!?" says his father, "No kidding! How do we get Ole' Blue into that program?" "Just send $2,500, and I'll get him into the class."

The money promptly arrives. But our hero has a problem.

At the end of the year, his father will find out the dog can neither talk, nor read. So he shoots the dog. When he arrives home at the end of the year, his father is all excited. "Where's Ole" Blue? I just can't wait to see him read something and talk!"

"Dad," the boy says, "I have some grim news. Yesterday morning, just before we left to drive home, Ole' Blue was in the living room, kicked back in the recliner, reading the National Post, like he usually does. Then Ole' Blue turned to me and asked, so, is your daddy still messing around with that little redhead who lives down the street?"

The father went white and exclaimed, "I hope you shot that son of a bitch before he talks to your Mother!"

"I sure did, Dad!"

"That's my boy!"

The kid went on to law school, and is now a politician seeking re-election.

⤸

JOAN, a rather well-proportioned and near-sighted secretary, spent almost all of her vacation sunbathing on the roof of her hotel. She wore a bathing suit the first few days, but always removed her glasses for an even facial tan. After several days she decided that no one could see her way up there, so she slipped out of her suit for an overall tan. She'd hardly begun when she heard someone running up the stairs; she was lying on her stomach, so she just pulled a towel over her rear.

"Excuse me, miss," said the flustered little assistant manager of the hotel, out of breath from running up the stairs. "The hotel doesn't mind your sunbathing on the roof, but we would very much appreciate your wearing a bathing suit as you have for the past week."

"What difference does it make?" Joan asked rather calmly. "No one can see me up here, and besides, I'm covered with a towel."

"Not exactly," said the embarrassed, little man. "You're lying on the dining room skylight!"

A group of fifteen-year-old girlfriends discussed where to meet for dinner. Finally, they agreed to meet at the Dairy Queen next to the Oceanview Restaurant because they had only six dollars among them and Jimmy Johnson, the cute boy in Social Studies, lived on that street.

Ten years later, the group of twenty-five-year-old girlfriends discussed where to meet for dinner. Finally, they agreed to meet at the Oceanview Restaurant because the beer was cheap, the restaurant offered free snacks, the band was good, there was no cover and there were lots of cute guys.

Ten years later, the group of thirty-five-year-old girlfriends discussed where to meet for dinner. Finally, they agreed to meet at the Oceanview Restaurant because the cosmos were good, it was right near the gym and, if they went late enough, there wouldn't be too many whiny little kids.

Ten years later, the group of forty-five-year-old girlfriends discussed where to meet for dinner. Finally, they agreed to meet at the Oceanview Restaurant because the martinis were big and the waiters had tight pants and nice buns.

Ten years later, the group of fifty-five-year-old girlfriends discussed where to meet for dinner. Finally, they agreed to meet at the Oceanview Restaurant because the prices were reasonable, the wine list was good, the restaurant had windows that opened (in case of a hot flash), and fish is good for cholesterol.

Ten years later, the group of sixty-five-year-old girlfriends discussed where to meet for dinner. Finally, they agreed to meet at the Oceanview Restaurant because the lighting was good and the restaurant had an early bird special.

Ten years later, the group of seventy-five-year-old girlfriends discussed where to meet for dinner. Finally, they agreed to meet at the Oceanview Restaurant because the food was not too spicy and the restaurant was handicapped-accessible.

Ten years later, the group of eight-five-year-old girlfriends discussed where to meet for dinner. Finally, they agreed to meet at the Oceanview Restaurant because they had never been there before.

PETER starts his new job at the London Zoo and is given three tasks. First is to clear the exotic fish pool of weeds. As he does this, a huge fish jumps out and bites him. To show who is boss, Peter beats it to death with a spade. Realizing his employer won't be best pleased; he disposes of the fish by feeding it to the lions, as lions will eat anything.

Moving on to the second job of cleaning up the chimp house, Peter is attacked by the chimps; they pelted him with coconuts. He swipes at two chimps with a spade killing them both. What can he do? Feed them to the lions, Peter says to himself, because lions eat anything. He hurls the corpses into the lion enclosure.

Peter moves on to his last job that is to collect honey from the South American Bees. As soon as he starts collecting the honey, he is attacked by a swarm of bees. He grabs the spade and smashes the swarm to a pulp. By now he knows what to do and throws them into the lion's cage because lions eat anything. Later that day a new lion arrives at the zoo. He wanders up to another lion and says, "What's the food like here?'"

The lion replies, "Absolutely brilliant! Today we had fish and chimps with mushy bees."

⤸

AT a high school in Saskatchewan, a group of boy students played a prank. They let three goats loose inside the school. Before turning them loose, they painted a number on the side of each goat, numbering them 1, 2, and 4... School administrators spent most of the day looking for goat number 3! Now that's funny, I don't care who you are...and you thought there was nothing to do in Saskatchewan!

⤸

AN actual sign posted at a golf club in Scotland, UK:

1. Back straight, knees bent, feet shoulder width apart
2. Form a loose grip
3. Keep your head down!
4. Avoid a quick back swing

5. Stay out of the water

6. Try not to hit anyone

7. If you are taking too long, let others go ahead of you

8. Don't stand directly in front of others

9. Quiet please...while others are preparing

10. Don't take extra strokes

Well done... now, flush the urinal. Go outside, and tee off.

⤸

A Scotsman and his wife walked past a swanky new restaurant. "Did you smell that food?" she asked, "Incredible!"

Being a kind-hearted Scotsman, he thought, "What the heck, I'll treat her!"

So, they walked past it again!

⤸

Two Jewish men, Sid and Al, were sitting in a Mexican restaurant. Sid asked Al, "I wonder if there are any people of our faith born and raised in Mexico?"

Al replied, "I don't know, let's ask our waiter." When the waiter came by, Al asked him, "Are there any Mexican Jews?"

The waiter said, "I don't know Senor, I'll ask the cooks." He returned from the kitchen in a few minutes and said "No, Senor, no Mexican Jews."

Al wasn't really satisfied with that and asked, "Are you absolutely sure?"

The waiter, realizing he was dealing with foreigners, gave the expected answer, "I will check again, Senor!" and went back into the kitchen.

While the waiter was away, Sid said, "I find it hard to believe that there are no Jews in Mexico, our people are scattered everywhere."

The waiter returned and said "Senor, the head cook said there is no Mexican Jews." "Are you certain?" Al asked once again. "I can't believe there are no Mexican Jews!"

"Senor, I ask EVERYONE," replied the exasperated waiter, "All we have is Orange Jews, Prune Jews, Tomato Jews, and Grape Jews."

A Modern Romance Novel

HE grasped me firmly, but gently, just above my elbow and guided me into a room; his room. Then he quietly shut the door and we were alone. He approached me soundlessly, from behind, and spoke in a low, reassuring voice, close to my ear.

"Just relax."

Without warning, he reached down and I felt his strong, calloused hands start at my ankles, gently probing and moving upward along my calves, slowly, but steadily. My breath caught in my throat. I knew I should be afraid, but somehow I didn't care. His touch was so experienced, so sure.

When his hands moved up onto my thighs, I gave a slight shudder, and I partly closed my eyes. My pulse was pounding. I felt his knowing fingers caress my abdomen, my ribcage. And then, as he cupped my firm, full breasts in his hands, I inhaled sharply.

Probing, searching, knowing what he wanted, he brought his hands to my shoulders, slid them down my tingling spine and into my panties.

Although I knew nothing about this man, I felt oddly trusting and expectant. This is a man, I thought. A man used to taking charge. A man not used to taking "no" for an answer. A man who would tell me what he wanted. A man who would look into my soul and say...

"Okay, ma"am," said a voice. "All done."

My eyes snapped open and he was standing in front of me, smiling, holding out my purse.

"You can board your flight now."

Each Friday night after work, Bubba would fire up his outdoor grill and cook a venison steak. But all of Bubba's neighbors were Catholic...and since it was Lent, they were forbidden from eating meat on Friday.

The delicious aroma from the grilled venison steaks was causing such a problem for the Catholic faithful that they finally talked to their Priest. The Priest came to visit Bubba, and suggested that he become a Catholic. After several classes and much study, Bubba attended Mass and as the Priest sprinkled holy water over him, he said, "You were born a Baptist, and raised a Baptist, but now you are a Catholic."

Bubba's neighbours were greatly relieved, until the first Friday night arrived, and the wonderful aroma of grilled venison filled the neighborhood. The neighbours immediately called the Priest and, as he rushed into Bubba's yard, clutching a rosary and prepared to scold him, he stopped and watched in amazement.

There stood Bubba, clutching a small bottle of holy water which he carefully sprinkled over the grilling meat and chanted: "You wuz born a deer, you wuz raised a deer, but now you is a catfish."

                         ⌣

On a transatlantic flight, a plane passes through a severe storm. The turbulence is awful, and things go from bad to worse when one wing is struck by lightning. One Irish woman (Spelly) in particular loses it. Screaming, she stands up in front of the plane.

"I'm too young to die!" Spelly wails. "Well, if I"m going to die, I want my last minutes on Earth to be memorable! I"ve had plenty of sex in my life, but no one has ever made me really feel like a woman! Well I've had it! Is there anyone on this plane who can make me feel like a woman?"

For a moment, there is silence. Everyone has forgotten their own peril, and they all stare, riveted, at the desperate Spelly in the front of the plane. Then, a man stands up in the rear of the plane.

"I can make you feel like a woman," he says. He's handsome. Tall, built, with long, flowing black hair and beautiful brown eyes, he starts to walk slowly up the aisle, unbuttoning his shirt one button at a time. No one moves.

Spelly is breathing heavily in anticipation as the stranger approaches. He removes his shirt. Muscles ripple across his chest as he reaches her; he extends his arm holding his shirt to the trembling woman, and whispers:

"Iron this, and then get me a beer."

⤴

WORKING people frequently ask retired people what they do to make their days interesting. Well, for example, the other day, Mary my wife and I went into town and visited a shop. When we came out, there was a cop writing out a parking ticket. We went up to him and I said, "Come on, man, how about giving a senior citizen a break?"

He ignored us and continued writing the ticket. I called him an "asshole." He glared at me and started writing another ticket for having worn-out tires. So Mary called him a "**** head." He finished writing out the second ticket and put it on the windshield along with the first. Then he started writing more tickets. This went on for about twenty minutes. The more we abused him, the more tickets he wrote.

Just then our bus arrived, and we got on it and went home. We try to have a little fun each day now that we're retired. It's important at our age.

⤴

FIVE pearls of Scottish wisdom to remember:

1. Money cannot buy happiness but, somehow, it's more comfortable to cry in a Mercedes Benz than it is on a bicycle.
2. Forgive your enemy but remember the bastard's name.
3. Help a man when he is in trouble and he will remember you when he is in trouble again.
4. Many people are alive only because it is illegal to shoot them.
5. Alcohol does not solve any problem, but neither does milk.

Why Our Health Care Costs Are So High

Bubba had shingles. Those of us who spend much time in a doctor's office should appreciate this! Doesn't it seem more and more that physicians are running their practices like an assembly line? Here's what happened to Bubba:

Bubba walked into a doctor's office and the receptionist asked him what he had. Bubba said: "Shingles."

So she wrote down his name, address, and medical insurance number and told him to have a seat.

Fifteen minutes later a nurse's aide came out and asked Bubba what he had.

Bubba said, "Shingles." So she wrote down his height, weight, a complete medical history and told Bubba to wait in the examining room.

A half hour later a nurse came in and asked Bubba what he had.

Bubba said, "Shingles."

So the nurse gave Bubba a blood test, a blood pressure test, an electrocardiogram, and told Bubba to take off all his clothes and wait for the doctor.

An hour later the doctor came in and found Bubba sitting patiently in the nude and asked Bubba what he had.

Bubba said, "Shingles."

The doctor asked, "Where?"

Bubba said, "Outside on the truck. Where do you want me to unload 'em?'

⌐

A young lady confidently walked around the room while leading a group seminar on stress management. When she raised glass of water, everyone knew she was going to ask the ultimate question, "half empty or half full?"

She fooled them all. "How heavy is this glass of water?" she inquired with a smile. Answers were called out and ranged from 8oz. to 20oz.

She replied, "The absolute weight doesn't matter. It depends on how long I hold it. If I hold it for a minute, that's not a problem. If I hold it for an hour, I'll have an ache in my right arm. If I hold it for a day, you'll have to call an ambulance. In each case it's the same weight, but the longer I hold it, the heavier it becomes."

She continued, "and that's the way it is with stress. If we carry our burdens all the time, sooner or later, as the burden becomes increasingly heavy, we won't be able to carry on."

"As with the glass of water, you have to put it down for a while and rest before holding it again. When we're refreshed, we can carry on with the burden—holding stress longer and better each time practiced. Life is short. Enjoy it and the now 'supposed' stress that you've conquered!"

Dealing With the Burdens of Life

1. Accept the fact that some days you're the pigeon—and some days you're the statue!
2. Always keep your words soft and sweet—just in case you have to eat them.
3. Always read stuff that will make you look good if you die in the middle of it.
4. Drive carefully—it's not just cars that can be recalled by their Maker.
5. If you can't be kind, at least have the decency to be vague.
6. If you lend someone $20 and never see that person again, it was probably worth it.
7. It may be that your sole purpose in life is simply to serve as a warning to others.
8. Never buy a car you can't push.
9. Never put both feet in your mouth at the same time, because then you won't have a leg to stand on.
10. Nobody cares if you can't dance well. Just get up and dance.
11. Since it's the early worm that gets eaten by the bird, sleep late.
12. The second mouse gets the cheese.

13. When everything's coming your way, you're in the wrong lane.

14. Birthdays are good for you. The more you have, the longer you live.

15. You may be only one person in the world, but you may also be the world to one person.

16. Some mistakes are too much fun to make only once.

17. We could learn a lot from crayons. Some are sharp, some are pretty and some are dull. Some have weird names and all are different colours—but they all have to live in the same box.

18. A truly happy person is one who can enjoy the scenery on a detour.

19. Have an awesome day and know that someone has thought about you today.

Layoff Letter

Dear Employees:

As the CEO of this organization, I have resigned myself to our current president because our taxes and government fees will increase in a big way. To compensate for these increases, our prices would have to increase by about 10%.

But, since we cannot increase our prices right now due to the dismal state of the economy, we will have to lay off sixty of our employees instead. This has really been bothering me since I believe we are family here and I didn't know how to choose who would have to go.

So, this is what I did. I walked through our parking lots and found sixty bumper stickers on our employees' cars with our President's name on it. I have decided these folks will be the ones to let go. I can't think of a more fair way to approach this problem. They voted for change...I gave it to them.

I will see the rest of you at the annual company picnic.

A drunken man walks into a biker bar, sits down at the bar and orders a drink.

Looking around, he sees three men sitting at a corner table. He gets up, staggers to the table, leans over, looks the biggest, meanest, biker in the face and says: "I went by your grandma's house today and I saw her in the hallway buck naked. Man, she is one fine looking woman!"

The biker looks at him and doesn't say a word. His buddies are confused, because he is one bad biker and would fight at the drop of a hat.

The drunk leans on the table again and says: "I got it on with your grandma and she is good, the best I ever had!"

The biker's buddies are starting to get really mad but the biker still says nothing.

The drunk leaned on the table one more time and said "I'll tell you something else, boy, your grandma liked it!"

At this point the biker stands up, takes the drunk by the shoulders looks him square in the eyes and says, "Grandpa, go home, you}re drunk."

Nine Things that will Disappear in our Lifetime

Some of these are not surprising and some are frightening.

1. **The Post Office**: Get ready to imagine a world without the post office. It is so deeply in financial trouble that there is probably no way to sustain it for the long term. E-mail, Fed Ex, and UPS have just about wiped out the minimum revenue needed to keep the Post Office alive. Most of your mail every day is junk mail and bills.

2. **The Cheque**: Britain is already laying the groundwork to do away with cheques by 2018. It costs the financial system billions of dollars a year to process cheques. Plastic cards and online transactions will lead to the eventual demise of the

cheque. This plays right into the death of the post office. If you never paid your bills by mail and never received them by mail, the Post Office would absolutely go out of business.

3. **The Newspaper**: The younger generation simply doesn't read the newspaper. They certainly don't subscribe to a daily delivered print edition. It may go the way of the milkman and the laundry man. The rise in mobile Internet devices and e-readers has caused the newspaper and magazine publishers to form an alliance. They have met with Apple, Amazon, and the major cell phone companies to develop a model for paid subscription internet connection services.

4. **The Book**: You say you will never give up the physical book that you hold in your hand and turn the literal pages. I said the same thing about downloading music from iTunes. I wanted my hard copy CD. But I quickly changed my mind when I discovered that I could get albums for half the price without ever leaving home to get the latest music. The same thing might happen with books. The internet price is less than half that of a real book.

5. **The Land Line Telephone**: Unless you have a large family and make a lot of local calls, you don't need a landline telephone anymore. Most people keep it simply because they've always had it. And it's much easier to hear voices on the landline phone.

6. **Music**: The music industry is dying a slow death. It's not just because of illegal downloading. It's the lack of innovative new music. Greed and corruption are the problems. The record labels and the radio conglomerates are simply self-destructing. Over 40% of the music purchased today is from "catalog items," meaning traditional music, older established artists that the public is familiar with.

7. **Television**: Revenues to the networks are down dramatically. People are watching TV and movies streamed from their computers. Prime time shows have degenerated down to lower than the lowest common denominator. Cable rates are skyrocketing and commercials run about every 4 minutes and 30 seconds. I say good riddance to most of it. It's time for the cable companies to be put out of our misery. Let the people choose what they want to watch online and through Netflix.

8. **"Things" That You Own**: Today your computer has a hard drive to store your pictures, music, movies, and documents. Your software is on a CD or DVD, and you can always re-install it if need be. But all of that is changing. Using the cloud system, when you turn on a computer, the Internet will be built into the operating system. If you click an icon, it will open something in the Internet cloud. If you save something, it will be saved to the cloud. And you may pay a monthly subscription fee to the cloud provider. Will you actually own any of this "stuff" or will it all be able to disappear at any moment in a big "Poof?" Will most of the things in our lives be disposable and whimsical?

9. **Privacy**: If ever there was a concept that we can look back on with nostalgia, it would be privacy. That's gone. It's been gone for a long time. There are cameras on the street, in most of the buildings, and even built into your computer and cell phone. But you can be sure that 24/7, "they" know who you are and where you are, right down to the GPS coordinates, and the Google Street View. If you buy something, your habit is put into a zillion profiles, and your ads will change to reflect those habits. And "they" will try to get you to buy something else. All we will have that can't be changed are memories.

One-Liners

- My neighbour knocked on my door at 2:30 this morning, can you believe that? 2:30 am! Luckily for him I was still playing my bagpipes.

- The Grim Reaper came for me last night, and I beat him off with a vacuum cleaner. Talk about Dyson with death.

- Paddy says, "Mick, I'm thinking of buying a Labrador." Mick replied, "Really? Have you seen how many of their owners go blind?"

- I saw a poor old lady fall over today on the ice! At least I presume she was poor—she only had $1.20 in her purse.

- My girlfriend thinks that I'm a stalker! Well, she's not exactly my girlfriend yet.

- I woke up last night to find the ghost of Gloria Gaynor standing at the foot of my bed. At first I was afraid, then I was petrified.

- The wife has been missing a week now. Police said to prepare for the worst, so I have been to the charity shop to get all her clothes back.

- A mate of mine admitted to being addicted to brake fluid. When I quizzed him on it, he reckoned he could stop any time.

- My daughter asked me for a pet spider for her birthday, so I went to our local pet shop and they were seventy dollars. I thought, "I can get one cheaper off the web."

- Statistically, six out of seven dwarves are not Happy.

- I was at an ATM yesterday when a little old lady asked if I could check her balance, so I pushed her over.

- I start a new job in Seoul next week. I thought it was a good Korea move.

- I was driving on the road this morning when I saw an AMA truck parked on the side of the road. The driver was sobbing uncontrollably and looked miserable. I thought to myself, "That guy is heading for a breakdown."

෨

Getting a Shave

AN old man walks into the barbershop for a shave and a haircut, but he tells the barber he can't get all his whiskers off because his cheeks are wrinkled from age.

The barber gets a little wooden ball from a cup on the shelf and tells him to put it inside his cheek to spread out the skin.

When he's finished, the old man tells the barber that was the cleanest shave he's had in years. But he wanted to know what would have happened if he had swallowed that little ball. The barber replied:

"You just bring it back tomorrow like everyone else does."

෨

Getting a Physical

AN old guy goes to his doctor for his physical and gets sent to the Urologist as a precaution. When he gets there, he discovers the Urologist is a very pretty female doctor.

The female doctor says, "I'm going to check your prostate today, but this new procedure is a little different from what you are probably used to. I want you to lie on your right side, bend your knees, and while I check your prostate, you take a deep breath and say, "99."

The old guy obeys and says, "99."

The doctor says, "Great". Now turn over on your left side and again, while I repeat the check, take a deep breath and say, "'99."

Again, the old guy says, "99."

The doctor said, "Very good." Now then, I want you to lie on your back with

your knees raised slightly. I'm going to check your prostate with this hand, and with the other hand I'm going to hold on to your penis to keep it out of the way. Now take a deep breath and say, '99'.

The old guy begins, "One …Two …Three…"

Irish Paddy Jokes

Paddy goes to the vet with his goldfish. "I think it's got epilepsy," he tells the vet.

The vet takes a look and says, "It seems calm enough to me."

Paddy says, "I haven't taken it out of the bowl yet."

Paddy spies a letter lying on his doormat. It says on the envelope "DO NOT BEND."

Paddy spends the next 2 hours trying to figure out how to pick the bloody thing up.

Paddy shouts frantically into the phone, "My wife is pregnant and her contractions are only two minutes apart!"

"Is this her first child?" asks the Doctor.

"No," shouts Paddy, "this is her husband!"

Paddy was driving home, drunk as a skunk, and suddenly he has to swerve to avoid a tree, then another, then another.

A cop car pulls him over as he veers about all over the road.

Paddy tells the cop about all the trees in the road.

The cop says, "For God's sake Paddy, that's your air freshener swinging about!"

An old Irish farmer's dog goes missing and he's inconsolable. His wife says, "Why don't you put an advert in the paper?"

He does, but two weeks later the dog is still missing.

"What did you put in the paper?," his wife asks.

"Here boy," he replies.

Paddy's in jail. Guard looks in his cell and sees him hanging by his feet.

"What the hell you doing?," he asks.

"Hanging myself," Paddy replies.

"It should be around your neck," says the Guard.

"I know," says Paddy, "but I couldn't breathe."

Father Norton

Father Norton woke up Sunday morning and realizing it was an exceptionally beautiful and sunny early spring day, decided he just had to play golf. He told the Associate Pastor that he was feeling sick and persuaded him to say Mass for him that day.

As soon as the Associate Pastor left the room, Father Norton headed out of town to a golf course about forty miles away. This way he knew he wouldn't accidentally meet anyone he knew from his parish. Setting up on the first tee, he was alone. After all, it was Sunday morning and everyone else was in church!

At about this time, Saint Peter leaned over to the Lord while looking down from the heavens and exclaimed, "You're not going to let him get away with this, are you?"

The Lord sighed, and said, "No, I guess not."

Just then Father Norton hit the ball and it shot straight towards the pin, dropping just short of it, rolled up and fell into the hole. It was a 420-yard hole in one!

St. Peter was astonished. He looked at the Lord and asked, "Why did you let him do that?"

The Lord smiled and replied, "Who's he going to tell?"

The Talking Centipede

Asingle guy decided life would be more fun if he had a pet. So he went to the pet store and told the owner that he wanted to buy an unusual pet.

After some discussion, he finally bought a talking centipede, a 100-legged critter that came with its own home — a little white box.

The guy took his new pet home and found a good spot for the box. He named his new pet "10 Cents" and decided he would start off by taking his new pet to church with him.

"Would you like to go to church with me today? We will have a good time."

But there was no answer from 10 Cents.

This bothered him a bit, but he waited a few minutes and then asked again, "How about going to church with me and receive blessings?"

But again, there was no answer from his new friend.

Now the guy is getting really worried. He waited a few minutes more, thinking about the situation. He decided to invite the centipede one last time.

This time he put his face up against the centipede's house and shouted, "Hey, in there! Would you like to go to church with me and learn about God?"

This time, a little voice came out of the box, "I heard you the first time! I've been putting on my shoes!"

~

Hot and Dry in Kansas

It's so hot Kansas...

- the birds have to use pot holders to pull the worms out of the ground.
- the trees are whistling for dogs.
- the best parking place is determined by shade instead of distance.

- hot water comes from both taps.
- you can make sun tea instantly.
- you learn that a seat buckle makes a pretty good branding iron.
- the temperature drops below 90 F and you feel a little chilly.
- you discover that in July it only takes two fingers to steer a car (one on each hand).
- you actually burn your hand opening the car door.
- you actually break into a sweat the instant you step outside at 5:30 am
- your biggest motorcycle wreck fear is, "what if I get knocked out and end up lying on the pavement and cook to death?"
- the potatoes cook underground, so all you have to do is pull one out and add butter.
- the cows are giving evaporated milk.
- farmers are feeding their chickens crushed ice to keep them from laying boiled eggs.

It's so dry in Kansas...

- that the Baptists are starting to baptize by sprinkling
- the Methodists are using wet wipes
- the Presbyterians are giving rain checks
- the Catholics are praying for wine to turn back into water

Places I Have Been

I have been in many places, but I've never been in Cahoots. Apparently, you can't go alone. You have to be in Cahoots with someone.

I've also never been in Cognito. I hear no one recognizes you there.

I have, however, been in Sane. They don't have an airport; you have to be driven there. I have made several trips there, thanks to my friends, family, and work.

I would like to go to Conclusions, but you have to jump, and I'm not too much on physical activity anymore.

I have also been in Doubt. That is a sad place to go, and I try not to visit there too often.

I've been in Flexible, but only when it was very important to stand firm.

Sometimes I'm in Capable, and I go there more often as I'm getting older.

One of my favorite places to be is in Suspense! It really gets the adrenalin flowing and pumps up the old heart! At my age I need all the stimuli I can get!

I may have been in Continent, and I don't remember what country I was in.

It's an age thing.

~

A Lesson in Irony

THE Food Stamp Program, administered by the U.S. Department of Agriculture, is proud to be distributing the greatest amount of free meals and food stamps ever.

Meanwhile, the National Park Service, administered by the U.S. Department of the Interior, asks us to "Please Do Not Feed the Animals."

Their stated reason for the policy is because the animals will grow dependent on handouts and will not learn to take care of themselves. This ends today's lesson.

~

Beer Call

I was standing in a bar in town yesterday and a little foreign man comes in, stands next to me and starts drinking a beer.

I said to him, "do you know any of those martial arts things, like Kung-Fu or Karate?"

He says, "No, why are you asking me that? Is it because you think I'm Chinese?"

"No," I say, "It's because you're drinking my beer you jerk."

⌇

Catholic Heart Attack

A man suffered a serious heart attack while shopping in a store. The store clerks called 911 when they saw him collapse to the floor.

The paramedics rushed the man to the nearest hospital where he had emergency open heart bypass surgery.

He awakened from the surgery to find himself in the care of nuns at the Catholic Hospital he was taken to. A nun was seated next to his bed holding a clipboard loaded with several forms, and a pen. She asked him how he was going to pay for his treatment.

"Do you have health insurance?" she asked.

He replied in a raspy voice, "No health insurance."

The nun asked, "Do you have money in the bank?"

He replied, "No money in the bank."

"Do you have a relative who could help you with the payments?" asked the irritated nun.

He said, "I only have a spinster sister, and she is a nun."

The nun became agitated and announced loudly, "Nuns are not spinsters! Nuns are married to God.[

The patient replied, "Perfect. Send the bill to my brother-in-law."

⌇

Mix-up

A blonde lady and a man are in an elevator. The blonde obviously just ending a hard day of work and says, "T.G.I.F."

The man sort of laughing and says, "S.H.I.T."

The lady frustrated says again, "T.G.I.F."

Again the man says, "S.H.I.T."

The lady turns to the man and says, "How dare you swear in the presence of a lady! T.G.I.F.! Thank God It's Friday."

The man turns to her and says, "I wasn't swearing! S.H.I.T. Sorry Honey It's Thursday."

~

The Wit of the Scots

A Greek and a Scotsman were sitting in a Starbuck's cafe one day discussing who had the superior culture. Over Triple lattes, the Greek guy says, "Well, we Greeks built the Parthenon," arching his eyebrows.

The Scotsman replies, "Well, it was the Scots that discovered the summer and winter Solstices."

The Greek retorts, "We Greeks gave birth to advanced mathematics."

The Scotsman nodded in agreement, says, "Scots were the first ones to discover timepieces and calendars."

And so on until the Greek comes up with what he thinks will end the discussion. With a flourish of finality he says, "The Greeks were the ones who invented sex!"

The Scotsman replies, "Indeed, that is true, but it was the Scots that introduced it to women."

~

The Origin of the Word "Olympics"

A slave call girl from Sardinia named Gedophamee was attending a great, but as yet, unnamed athletic festival 2500 years ago in Greece.

In those days, believe it or not, the athletes performed naked.

To prevent unwanted arousal while competing, the men imbibed freely on drink containing saltpeter before and throughout the variety of events.

At the opening ceremonial parade Gedophamee observed the first wave of naked magnificent males marching toward her and she exclaimed: "Oh! Limp Pricks!"

Over the next two and a half millennia that morphed into "Olympics."

⌒

Elderly Couple Road Trip

WHILE on a road trip, an elderly couple stopped at a roadside restaurant for lunch. After finishing their meal, they left the restaurant and resumed their trip. When leaving, the elderly woman unknowingly left her glasses on the table and she didn't miss them until they had been driving about twenty minutes.

By then, to add to the aggravation, they had to travel quite a distance before they could find a place to turn around—in order to return to the restaurant to retrieve her glasses. All the way back, the husband became the classic grouchy old man.

He fussed and complained and scolded his wife relentlessly during the entire return drive. The more he chided her, the more agitated he became. He just wouldn't let up.

To her relief, they finally arrived at the restaurant. As the woman got out of the car and hurried inside to retrieve her glasses, the old geezer yelled to her, "While you're in there, you might as well get my hat and the credit card!"

⌒

Owner of the Bar

AN Arab walks into a bar and is about to order a drink when he sees a guy close by wearing a Jewish cap, a prayer shawl/tzitzis and traditional locks of hair. He doesn't have to be an Einstein to know that this guy is Jewish.

So, he shouts over to the bartender so loudly that everyone can hear, "Drinks for everyone in here, bartender, but not for that Jew over there."

Soon after the drinks have been handed out, the Jew gives him a big smile, waves at him, then says, "Thank you!" in an equally loud voice. This infuriates the Arab. He once again loudly orders drinks for everyone except the Jew.

As before, this does not seem to bother the Jewish guy. He continues to smile, and again yells, "Thank you!"

The Arab asks the bartender, "What's the hell is the matter with that Jew? I've ordered two rounds of drinks for everyone in the bar but him, and all the silly bugger does is smile and thank me. Is he nuts?"

"Nope," replies the bartender. "He owns the place."

Punographics

- When chemists die, they barium.
- Jokes about German sausage are the wurst.
- I know a guy who's addicted to brake fluid. He says he can stop any time.
- How does Moses make his tea? Hebrews it.
- I stayed up all night to see where the sun went. Then it dawned on me.
- This girl said she recognized me from the vegetarian club, but I'd never met herbivore.
- I'm reading a book about anti-gravity. I just can't put it down.
- I did a theatrical performance about puns. It was a play on words.
- They told me I had type A blood, but it was a Type-O.
- Why were the Indians here first? They had reservations.
- We are going on a class trip to the Coca-Cola factory. I hope there's no pop quiz.
- I didn't like my beard at first. Then it grew on me.
- Did you hear about the cross-eyed teacher who lost her job because she couldn't control her pupils?

- When you get a bladder infection, urine trouble.
- Broken pencils are pointless.
- I tried to catch some fog, but I mist.
- What do you call a dinosaur with an extensive vocabulary? A thesaurus.
- England has no kidney bank, but it does have a Liverpool.
- I used to be a banker, but then I lost interest.
- I dropped out of communism class because of lousy Marx.
- All the toilets in New York's police stations have been stolen. The police have nothing to go on.
- I got a job at a bakery because I kneaded dough.
- Velcro—what a rip off!
- A cartoonist was found dead in his home. Details are sketchy.
- Venison for dinner again? Oh deer!
- The earthquake in Washington obviously was the government's fault.
- Be kind to your dentist. He has fillings, too.

The Official Redneck Dictionary

Rednecks have the lowest stress rate of us all because they do not take medical terminology seriously. You are going to die anyway, so live life.

- **Artery**: The study of paintings
- **Bacteria**: Back door to cafeteria
- **Barium**: What doctors do when patients die
- **Benign**: What you be, after you be eight
- **Caesarean**: Section A neighborhood in Rome
- **Cat scan**: Searching for Kitty
- **Cauterize**: Made eye contact with her
- **Colic**: A sheep dog
- **Coma**: A punctuation mark
- **Dilate**: To live long
- **Enema**: Not a friend

- **Fester**: Quicker than someone else
- **Fibula**: A small lie
- **Impotent**: Distinguished, well known
- **Labour Pain**: Getting hurt at work
- **Medical Staff**: A Doctor's cane
- **Morbid**: A higher offer
- **Nitrates**: Cheaper than day rates
- **Node**: I knew it
- **Outpatient**: A person who has fainted
- **Pelvis**: Second cousin to Elvis
- **Post Operative**: A letter carrier
- **Recovery Room**: Place to do upholstery
- **Rectum**: Nearly killed him
- **Secretion**: Hiding something
- **Seizure**: Roman emperor
- **Tablet**: A small table
- **Terminal Illness**: Getting sick at the airport
- **Tumor**: One plus one more
- **Urine**: Opposite of you're out

Where to Live When You Retire

No nursing home for us. We're checking into the Holiday Inn! With the average cost for a nursing home care costing $188.00 per day, there is a better way when we get old and feeble. We have already checked on reservations at the Holiday Inn.

For a combined long-term stay discount and senior citizen discount, it's $49.23 per night. That leaves $138.77 a day for: breakfast, lunch and dinner in any restaurant we want, or room service, laundry, gratuities and special TV movies.

Plus, they provide a swimming pool, a workout room, a lounge and washer-dryer. Most have free toothpaste and razors, and all have free shampoo and soap.

$5 worth of tips a day will have the entire staff scrambling to help you. They treat you like a customer, not a patient.

There is a city bus stop out front, and seniors ride free. The handicap bus will also pick you up (if you fake a decent limp).

To meet other nice people, call a church bus on Sundays.

For a change of scenery, take the airport shuttle bus and eat at one of the nice restaurants there. While you're at the airport, fly somewhere. Otherwise, the cash keeps building up.

It takes months to get into decent nursing homes. Holiday Inn will take your reservation today. And you are not stuck in one place forever, you can move from Inn to Inn, or even from city to city.

Want to see Hawaii? They have a Holiday Inn there too.

TV broken? Light bulbs need changing? Need a mattress replaced? No problem. They fix everything, and apologize for the inconvenience.

The Inn has a night security person and daily room service. The maid checks to see if you are okay. If not, they will call the undertaker or an ambulance. If you fall and break a hip, Medicare will pay for the hip, and Holiday Inn will upgrade you to a suite for the rest of your life.

And no worries about visits from family. They will always be glad to find you, and probably check in for a few days mini-vacation. Or, the kids could pay for a nursing home policy to protect their inheritance. (Never understood why we save so that they can have more. Thought that is why we paid for college—so they could provide for themselves.)

The grand kids can use the pool.

What more can you ask for? So, when we reach that golden age, we'll face it with a grin.

⌒

Senior citizens are the nation's leading carriers of aids!

- Hearing aids
- Band aids
- Roll aids
- Walking aids
- Medical aids

- Government aids
- Most of all, Monetary aid to their kids!
- Not forgetting HIV (Hair is Vanishing)

⌐⌐

A Blonde in Church

AN Alabama pastor said to his congregation, "Someone in this congregation has spread a rumour that I belong to the Ku Klux Klan. This is a horrible lie and one that a Christian community cannot tolerate. I am embarrassed and do not intend to accept this. Now, I want the party who said this to stand and ask forgiveness from God and this Christian family."

The preacher continued, "Do you have the nerve to face me and admit this is a falsehood? Remember, you will be forgiven and in your heart you will feel glory. Now stand and confess your transgression."

Again, all was quiet.

Then, slowly, a drop-dead gorgeous blonde with a body that would stop a runaway train rose from the third pew.

Her head was bowed and her voice quivered as she spoke, "Reverend there has been a terrible misunderstanding. I never said you were a member of the Ku Klux Klan, I simply told a couple of my friends that you were a wizard under the sheets."

⌐⌐

Telephone Tower

THREE Newfies were working at the top of a phone tower. As they start their descent, Jim slips, falls off the tower, and is killed instantly.

As the ambulance takes the body away, John says, "Well, shit, someone's gotta go and tell Jim's wife."

Joe says, "OK, I'm pretty good at that sensitive stuff, I'll do it."

Two hours later, he comes back carrying a case of Beer.

John says, "Where'd you get the beer, Joe?"

"Jim's wife gave it to me," Joe replies.

"That's unbelievable, you told the Missus her husband was dead and she gave you a case of beer?'

"Well, not exactly," Joe says. "When she answered the door, I said to her, 'you must be Jim's widow.'"

She said, "You must be mistaken. I'm not a widow."

Then I said, "I'll bet you a case of beer you are."

Newfies are good at that sensitive stuff.

~

Irish Golf Joke

A golfer playing in Ireland hooked his drive into the woods. Looking for his ball, he found a little Leprechaun flat on his back, a big bump on his head and his golf ball beside him. Horrified, the golfer got his water bottle from the cart and poured it over the little guy, reviving him.

"Arrgh! What happened?," the Leprechaun asked.

"I'm afraid I hit you with my golf ball," the golfer says.

"Oh, I see. Well, ye got me fair and square. Ye get three wishes, so whaddya want?"

"Thank God, you're all right!," the golfer answers in relief. "I don't want anything, I'm just glad you're OK, and I apologize."

And the golfer walks off.

"What a nice guy," the Leprechaun says to himself. "I have to do something for him. I'll give him the three things I would want...a great golf game, all the money he ever needs, and a fantastic sex life."

A year goes by and the golfer is back. On the same hole, he again hits a bad drive into the woods and the Leprechaun is there waiting for him.

"Twas me that made ye hit the ball here," the little guy says. "I just want to ask ye, how's yer golf game?"

"My game is fantastic!," the golfer answers. "I'm an internationally famous golfer now." He adds, "By the way, it's good to see you're all right."

"Oh, I'm fine now, thank ye. I did that fer yer golf game, you know. And tell me, how's yer money situation?"

"Why, it's just wonderful!," the golfer states. "When I need cash, I just reach in my pocket and pull out $100 bills I didn't even know were there!"

"I did that fer ye also. And tell me, how's yer sex life?"

The golfer blushes, turns his head away in embarrassment, and says shyly, "It's OK."

"C'mon, c'mon now," urged the Leprechaun, "I'm wanting to know if I did a good job. How many times a week?"

Blushing even more, the golfer looks around then whispers, "Once, sometimes twice a week."

"What?," responds the Leprechaun in shock. "That's all? Only once or twice a week?"

"Well," says the golfer, "I figure that's not bad for a Professor in a small college."

⤸

Mother Attends the Game

At one point during a game, the coach said to one of his young players,

"Do you understand what cooperation is? What a team is?"

The little boy nodded in the affirmative.

"Do you understand that what matters is whether we win together as a team?[

The little boy nodded yes.

"So," the coach continued, "when a strike is called, or you're out at first, you don't argue or curse or attack the umpire. Do you understand all that?"

Again the little boy nodded.

"Good," said the coach. "Now go over there and explain it to your mother."

A Young Farm Couple

A young farm couple, Homer and Darlene, got married and just couldn't seem to get enough lovin'. In the morning, before Homer left the house for the fields, they made love. When Homer came back from the fields, they made love. And again at bedtime, they made love.

The problem was their nooner; it took Homer a half hour to travel home and another half hour to return to the fields and he just wasn't getting enough work done. Finally Homer asked the town doctor what to do.

"Homer," said the doctor, "just take your rifle out to the field with you and when you're in the mood, fire off a shot into the air. That will be Darlene's signal to come out to you. Then you won't lose any field time."

They tried Doc's advice and it worked well for a while. Homer came back to the doctor's office.

"What's wrong?," asked the Doc. "Didn't my idea work?"

"Oh, it worked real good," said Homer. "Whenever I was in the mood, I fired off a shot like you said and Darlene'd come runnin'. We'd find a secluded place, make love, and then she'd go back home again."

"Good, Homer. So what's the problem?," asked the Doc.

"I ain't seen her since huntin' season started."

Sunbathing

A widowed lady, still in good shape, was sunbathing on a totally deserted beach at Ft. Myers. She looked up and noticed that a man her age, also in good shape, had walked up, placed his blanket on the sand near hers and began reading a book. Smiling, she attempted to strike up a conversation with him.

"How are you today?"

"Fine, thank you," he responded, and turned back to his book.

"I love the beach. Do you come here often?," she asked.

"First time since my wife passed away 2 years ago," he replied and turned back to his book.

"I'm sorry to hear that. My husband passed away three years ago and it is very lonely," she countered. "Do you live around here?" She asked.

"Yes, I live over in Cape Coral," he answered, and again he resumed reading.

Trying to find a topic of common interest, she persisted, "Do you like pussy cats?"

With that, the man dropped his book, came over to her blanket, tore off her swimsuit and gave her the most passionate lovemaking of her life.

When the cloud of sand began to settle, she gasped and asked the man, "How did you know that was what I wanted?"

The man replied, "How did you know my name was Katz?"

About the Book

THIS book contains all you need to know about sales, marketing, public speaking, and what you need to say to close a successful deal.

Marton Murphy started his working life with just a few hundred dollars to his name. Even though he did not have much formal education, had a speech impediment, and felt unable to speak in public, he acquired and made good use of the skills outlined in this book to overcome any and all obstacles that might otherwise have prevented him from being successful in life. Over the years, these same skills enabled Marton to become a multi-millionaire, a journey that is shared in his first book, *Misfortune to Multi-Millionaire*, published in 2012.

Individuals who wish to be successful in their conversational skills and in sales and marketing or simply seek to lead a successful life—in business or otherwise—should read *Misfortune to Multi-Millionaire*.

If you are interested in becoming an associate author with Notram Publishing or in learning how to write and publish a book, please contact **marton.murphy@hotmail.com.**

About the Author

MARTON MURPHY began his working life a chore boy, potato picker, and blacksmith's helper on Prince Edward Island. Marton Murphy found Prince Edward Island to be one of the nicest places in the world during the summer, with blue skies, blue water, red soil, green grass, colourful houses and barns, and beautiful boats in harbours.

He left PEI when he was 18 years old to hitchhike to Alberta, but wound up walking a large part of the way. In a little over a month, he arrived in Ontario where he weeded strawberries, and picked cherries, peaches, and tobacco. With what he earned in the fields, he purchased a car and drove it to Alberta, selling it for twice the price he had originally paid for it. In Alberta, Marton worked as a roughneck, welder, mechanic, and catskinner in both the oilfield and construction businesses. At various times, he also worked as a cowboy and taxi driver.

For a period of ten years he was employed by a large international company and subsequently started his first business enterprises—in the oilfield during the winters and in construction during the summers. He achieved all of this while serving in a voluntary capacity in his community, his church, and with charitable groups across Canada. He also found time to play a significant background role in politics at the local, regional, and national level.

Over the course of a working lifetime—of more than five decades— Marton Murphy has successfully climbed to the top of the corporate ladder. During his ascent, he has expanded his business interests and empire from activities in the oilfield and construction industry, into land, cattle, engineering, contracting, manufacturing, distribution, transportation, and travel.

He is an inventor and entrepreneur, philanthropist, political activist, environmentalist, adventurer, sportsman, builder, traveller, and author.

Individuals who wish to be successful in their conversational skills and in sales and marketing or simply seek to lead a successful life—in business or otherwise—should readMarton's first book, *Misfortune to Multi-Millionaire*.

If you are interested in becoming an associate author with Notram Publishing or in learning how to write and publish a book, please contact **marton.murphy@hotmail.com.**